Cornish Cookery

Cornish Cookery

Recipes of Today and Yesteryear

Vida Heard

DYLLANSOW TRURAN

First published in 1984
By Dyllansow Truran
Trewolsta, Trewirgie, Kernow (Cornwall)

Copyright © 1984 Vida Heard

Printed in Great Britain
Printed and Bound by Troutbeck Press, a subsidiary of R Booth (Bookbinder) Limited
Antron Hill, Mabe, Penryn, Cornwall.
Typeset and Cover Design by Delta Graphics
ISBN 0 907566 91 X

This is for Norma, my sister,
who I met again in Cornwall,
after many years.

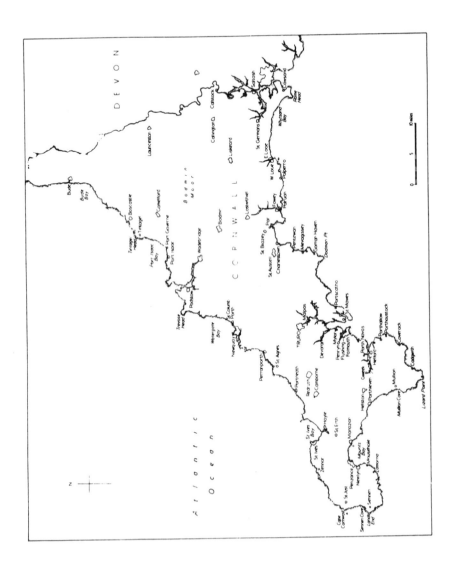

6

Contents

BEHIND IT ALL

'I was eatin' fair maidens and drinkin' mahogany.'

The seaman from Looe who said this to establish an alibi was fully understood by the Cornish folk in the courtroom, yet the judge and learned counsel at the Assizes were baffled, and had to call in an interpreter.

'The fairmaids m'lud are salted pilchards and the mahogany, called blackstrap by some, is a mixture of treacle and gin.'

Well, to this day visitors are often at a loss to understand Cornish talk and even learning the language (now taught to 250 children in the schools) does not mean you will be able to understand the lingo of the countryside. Having lived over fifty years abroad, I have difficulty in understanding some of the people on our Portscatho to Truro bus. Yet their expressions seem to have the art of creaming off the milk of language into words of their own choice; uplifting and endearing. For example, smuggling is known as fair trading and the man selling fish or vegetables addresses any old hag as 'me luv or luveur' and her spouse, dog or grandson as 'me andsome'.

A Cornish friend suggests that the politeness of the *'wern'* (Cornish folk) is rather like a fire-shield to protect them from the unpleasant realities of life. And who objects? My daughter-in-law's father from South Africa was so overcome by his landlady calling him her 'luveur' he never misses crossing the Tamar when he visits Britain.

After half a lifetime in Southern Africa, I returned for retirement in this village where I happen to be the last survivor of the oldest family; I had no idea when I came that I was. Also I had no idea when I bought the flat at the edge of Gerrans Bay that an ancestor was drowned pilchard-fishing in that very bay in 1650 — two years before Jan van Riebeeck started a white settlement in the Cape and ate his first meal of hippo meat.

I returned with a handicap — knowing next to nothing about Cornwall, our history, our food. Picking up the past, curious as ever about how the average working families lived — reading, questioning, checking — it was an easier task than when I researched for *Cookery in Southern Africa*. For one thing there are copious records here, while in South Africa after travelling thousands of miles to tribal territories and visiting all the Republic's many museums to dig out recipes brought by the settlers, I found the curator's answers disappointing. Huguenot recipes apparently did not exist because when these persecuted Frenchmen arrived in the 17th century (and started the Cape's viticulture) they were not allowed to write in French and most French records were destroyed.

The 1820 British immigrants to the Eastern Cape had left nothing because of burnings during the Kaffir Wars which ravaged that area in the last century. The 1850 settlers in Natal had left practically no recipes 'because the cockroaches had eaten them'! And so on. With few records to help, the jigsaw of fact, myth and legend had to be sorted out.

But here in Cornwall with a multitude of valuable records, there were still myths among facts, and fallacies too, concerning the food of our ancestors; and readers may disagree with my findings.

The incursions into my life abroad make this a rather personal book but, as merely one of many who have returned to roots with a greater appreciation of Cornwall and its heritage, I am hoping others will take over where I have left off. After all, man has marched through history on his stomach, but precious little has been told about the actual food history of the average working families, be they farmers, labourers, miners, fishermen. The groaning tables of the gentry are noticeably missing in these pages, so much has already been written about them.

The contents of this small book, bursting at its seams with an overflow of stories and recipes yet to be published in a further book may give to some an inordinate emphasis on fish. This is purposeful for I truly believe that we in Cornwall are at last realising our potential from the fish caught near our own shores. For one, I have a competition in mind for our restaurants to popularise our wealth of sea food. But that's another story!

ALL RIGHT?

The Metric Mix-up

All right? This kindly greeting, surely the best in the world, sums up the caring attitude of us Cornish for 'One and All', the motto on the Cornish coat of arms. I am hoping that the reader will regard the foust of Metric and Imperial measures in these pages with as generous an attitude. A book of this kind, using ancient and modern recipes, cannot conform to the usual cook-book presentation. The old recipes with Imperial measures must be printed as they were originally. The modern ones or old ones applicable for use today follow the Metric with Imperial measures in parenthesis. But the snag here is that there are two schools of thought — just as there are in the side and middle crimping of pasties. For example, some cook books choose to follow the easy all-round conversion of one ounce, the 25 g unit to the alternative 30 g unit. The true conversion being 28.350 g, it would involve us in unrealistic calculations. The Metric authorities suggest we take our pick of the higher or lower conversion, but naturally stick to it throughout.

Although it is preferable to follow one or other of the conversion methods I have been faced with the problem of not changing some of the tested recipes given me for inclusion in this book. But care has been taken to follow which ever alternative the writer has chosen throughout the given recipes. To ease the reading of recipes, spoons and cups have been printed without the Metric equivalent. This book is not a standard textbook on cookery (although my several former cordon bleu books were). It is essential, however, for the reader to refer to the measures given for cups and spoons just before the Index, at least when following modern recipes. As for the older recipes, it was customary to use a breakfast-size cup and, when a glass is mentioned, the old fashioned big tumbler was intended. Please refer to *Measure for Measure* at the end of this book.

BROTHS AND POTTAGES

Hereabouts some people still use the word broth in preference to soup and in olden times this was varied with 'mess' and 'pottage'. Messes? No wonder, when we read about the old ale-house soups, and in particular what mess of pottage Kiddleywink broth must have been.

Reading old Cornish cook books, I am not the only one who has wrestled with the meaning of kiddleywink. The origin of this term for ale-houses without full license is obscure and we are fobbed off with: as the ale-house keeper kept smuggled brandy in a kettle, those customers in the know would wink in the direction of the kettle. Or, there was a man named Winkle who started off the kiddley subterfuge.

My curiosity was aroused so I looked up the old word for kettle, knowing full well that a cauldron or cooking jar was a kettle in the old days. But under that expression 'kettle of fish' is given in my encyclopaedia 'kiddle of fish'. Kiddle, it explains, was a trap placed in the mouth of rivers to ensnare fish. This trap was illegal. The poaching of fish was a highly punishable offence. Was the kiddleywink possibly so named because it also was illegal, and the word kiddley linked to wink meaning a 'corner' as it is in Germanic languages or 'shop' as winkel means in South African Afrikaans? (Afrikaans having been evolved from Dutch.) Illegal corner or illegal shop, to my mind, is more plausible than the other explanations I have read. But this theory is for you, my readers, to explore or explode. It is just an idea that may fizzle out, as so many ideas do when we try to get to the roots of Celtic words and expressions.

Talking of kettles, labouring men enjoyed heating up their ale or cider in a kettle (pot) for a warm drink with sugar, or plunging a hot poker into the tankard to do likewise. Soups were often laced with alcohol — reminding us of our refinement with sherry today — but even porridges and gruels could be tiddley drinks.

Kiddleywink Soup

Yes, it shocks us all. To think that anyone could have been so hungry to imbibe it is distressing, but then Blue Line and Sinkers was almost worse, as will be seen further on. The explanation must be that the kiddleywink had to provide something to fill alcohol-enfeebled stomachs and at a minimum cost. (The poor creatures had spent their all on illicit brandy, rum or maybe geneva or gin.) But here, for the curious, is the recipe for this lowest soup of all. It might be said to be the poorest relation of the French onion soups, those superb 'hangover specials', and noticeably onion juice is there. Onion, garlic, leeks; what would the history of cooking be without them?

Kiddley or kettle broth basically was merely bread off-cuts over which some seasoned onion water was thrown to soften the crusts. Sometimes a few marigold leaves were thrown on top of the soup and/or the chopped leaves of wild leek. This common plant looks like a white bluebell with three-cornered leaves and a taste similar to wild garlic. Dripping and bacon rinds might find their way into a kiddley broth in the early 19th century and one recipe suggests that a few snails be thrown in for good measure. This form of cheap protein was presumably a coastal contribution of sea snails and not supplied by garden snails.

Winkles make a good shellfish soup, very easy to make as the winkles do not have to be freed from their shells in this old recipe. Even the gentry enjoyed this soup on occasions, maybe because some wine, cider or ale was thrown into the tureen and the hot winkle soup poured on top.

Winkle Soup

Half a bucketful of limpets or periwinkles are put into fresh water to cleanse and kill them. Scrape the shells clean, pound the creatures (shell and all) with a pestle and mortar, cover with water and boil. When done, strain through a cloth and add beef or mutton stock in which an onion has been boiled, in the proportion of one cup to every 3 cups of periwinkle broth. Boil up the liquid with one dozen peppercorns, allspice, a tablespoon of burnt sugar, thickening with one tablespoon of flour. Serve with cider or wine as above.

Morgay Soup

Among the stomach-filling broths of our past is the colourfully named Morgay Soup (Cornish *mor*, sea: *ky*, dog) and made as its name implied from dog fish, which reminds me a fish wholesaler told me used to be sold by the ton to London fish and chip shops.

Before the recipes for more palatable fare and not to miss out on the record of poverty-stricken broths of even less than a hundred years ago, here are two classic Cornish horrors!

Sky-Blue and Sinkers

It may be difficult to believe that such anaemic broths were served within living memory. Shirley (see acknowledgements at front of book) says she remembers her grandfather enjoying kiddley broth before going to bed right up to the time of his death at 85 (now 30 years since my writing this). He also enjoyed his 'sky-blue and sinkers', made with scalded milk, bread and sugar at breakfast. The following recipe is included in that invaluable collection of recipes compiled by Edith Martin and issued by the Cornwall Federation of Women's Institutes in 1929:

Into a three-legged crock fixed over a brisk fire of furze and turf, was poured a quantity of water. While this was reaching boiling point, some flour, usually barley, was mixed in a basin with scalded milk. This was emptied into the water in the crock and allowed to

14

boil for a minute or two. Next it was poured into basins into which 'sops' of barley bread had been put. These sops sank to the bottom, nothing being visible but the liquid, light blue in colour — hence the sobriquet 'sky-blue and sinkers'. It was eaten with an iron spoon.

Gerty Grey

Taking the place of bread and milk, this depended on flour and water kept quite thin — possibly if thicker you would be eating glue! Two nonsensical sayings arose from Gerty Grey. A man hacking old stumps would say: 'Gerty Grey, if you won't come up, there you may stay.' Or 'Gerty milk, if you won't come up I'll break the hilt.'

Beer or Ale Soup

Left-over ale was used for soups and even now if you find you have some beer over, it may be added to your home-made soup. It matters not a drop if it be flat.

After washing 50 g (2 oz) of sago in cold water, drain and boil it in 6 cups of not-too-bitter ale, add ½ lemon and a few cloves of cinnamon to taste. Boil for 20 minutes, strain, heat up and add a little thinly-sliced lemon rind and a glass of brandy or rum for six servings.

Nettle Soup

A Spring Tonic

Many women remember collecting nettles in the last war, for cooking like spinach or making into soup. All you need is a pair of rubber gloves to pick and prepare them; the stinging hairs disappear while they are boiling. The following recipe includes a few leaves of sorrel, but these may be omitted.

450 g (1 lb) nettle tops, a few leaves of sorrel, 1 onion, 25 g (1 oz) butter, 900 ml (1½ pints stock or chicken cubes in water), ½ teaspoon lemon juice, 1 tablespoon flour, 2 tablespoons cream, salt and pepper.

After chopping the nettles, sorrel and onion, put all into a large saucepan with the butter and cook for 10 minutes. Now add the stock, lemon juice and seasoning. Simmer until the vegetables are really soft. Mix flour or cornflour with a little water, stirring until the soup has thickened. Fold in the cream before serving.

Flatpoll Soup

Cabbage was a welcome filler for soups and stews in even recent times, in particular that common flat white cabbage known as 'flat poll'. Cooks 'in service' in their youth tell me that any meat from hen to pork or ham was cooked with the quartered cabbage with added stock and seasoning. It was a hearty supper for farmers who ignored the fact they grew those flatpolls as fodder crop for their animals.

Dried Bean and Pea Soups

Dried pea and bean soups are made by soaking overnight and simmering with seasoning, onion, and other vegetables in water next day. Add pieces of frizzled bacon or ham and serve with croutons of fried bread. Tomatoes are good in bean soup — but remember that vital teaspoon of sugar.

Vegetable Soups

All the vegetable soups, such as sorrel, lettuce, cabbage and the roots, such as artichokes, potato, cauliflower, carrot and mushrooms, are easy to make using the modern blender method, which ensures you do not waste a bud or leaf. It is also applicable to fruit soups which are so sadly neglected, I feel, because hot or chilled with a blob of Cornish cream they can be fit for the gods.

Fruit Soups

Fruit for soups — hot and cold — should be simmered until soft with water and sugar to taste, then strained. A little spice such as cinnamon, ginger or nutmeg or thinly peeled rind of lemon or orange can be added for distinctive flavours. A few drops of fresh lemon juice invariably improves a fruit soup. When thickening is required use fine sago, tapioca, cornflour or arrowroot in preference to flour, just as you do for fruit pies.

Rhubarb Soup

Savoury

Among the simple fruit soups from your garden is a savoury one, which needs only the following:

6 sticks of young rhubarb, about 1 litre (2 pints) good beef or veal or chicken stock, 1 medium onion, 2 thin slices of bread, salt and pepper. (Serves 5.)

Cut peeled rhubarb into short lengths. Throw into the stock and add the onion, bread and seasoning. Boil, skimming at intervals the scum as it rises. When rhubarb is tender, strain and serve with toasted sippets.

Curried Apple Soup

Two tablespoons butter, 1 large onion, coarsely chopped, 2 cups chicken stock (or use chicken stock cubes), 1/3 cup water, 1 tablespoon good curry powder, 1 tablespoon cornflour, 2 egg yolks, 1/2 cup cream, 2 tasty apples (such as Bramley), a dash of soy sauce, salt and pepper, juice of 1/2 lemon, watercress for garnish.

Melt butter, add chopped onion and cook until soft, but not brown. Stir in the chicken stock, water and curry powder. Add cornflour mixed with a little water. Bring to the boil and then simmer for 8 minutes. Add egg yolks to the cream and stir gradually into the hot soup, removing from the heat. Transfer mixture to an electric blender with an apple, peeled, cored and sliced. Blend until smooth or pass through a fine sieve. Season to taste with salt, pepper and soy sauce. Peel, core and dice remaining apple and marinate in lemon juice to retain colour. Just before serving stir in the diced apple and watercress leaves to garnish. Serves 4.

Bouillabaise

Cornish Version

This mediterranean soup is an example of millionaire fare inspired by the lowliest fisherman's food, which actually can contain anything seaworthy, including his bait.

Fish stock (from head, bones and skin), pieces of cooked fish, ½ teaspoon chopped garlic, 1 teaspoon dried thyme, a finger-length strip orange peel, 1 bay leaf or lemon leaf, ¼ teaspoon crushed saffron or turmeric, a drop of tabasco sauce, hot tomato sauce.

Simmer all ingredients in the fish stock, then strain and add a spoon of cream if liked. Pour the soup into individual hot soup bowls until ⅔ full. Pile in the centre of each bowl small pieces of neatly cut up seasoned fish with a shrimp or two if available. Hand round hot tomato sauce to which you have added tiny cubes of chopped green peppers.

Truly French Onion Soup

Traditional Hangover Special

50 g (2 oz) butter, 2 tablespoons cooking oil, 1 kg (2 lb) onion, 1 teaspoon salt, ½ teaspoon sugar, 25 g (1 oz) flour, 2 litres (4 pints) seasoned stock (or equivalent using chicken cubes with water).

Melt butter and oil in a large saucepan. Keeping the heat low, stir in onion, salt and sugar; stir occasionally until onions are a golden brown, which should be in about 20 minutes. Sprinkle the flour over the onions and stir for 2 or 3 minutes. Remove pan from heat. Bring the stock to simmering point in a separate saucepan, then stir the hot stock into the onions. Simmer soup, covered, for about half an hour, occasionally skimming off scum or fat. Taste for seasoning.

Onion Soup Gratinée

To make the above soup gratinée: Preheat oven to 190°C (375°F). Pour onion soup into a heat-proof tureen or individual soup bowls. Top with croutons made as follows: spread 12 slices of French bread (1″ thick) on a baking sheet in the oven at 160°C (325°F) for 15 minutes. With a pastry brush lightly coat both sides of each slice with olive oil. Turn the slices and bake for another 15 minutes until the bread is completely dry and a pale brown colour. Rub each slice with a cut clove of garlic and set aside. Sprinkle grated cheese with a little melted butter on top of each and put in the oven for five minutes until cheese has melted. Place the croutons on top of the soup and slide the soup under a hot grill for a minute.

SEAFOOD

Fish from the Sea

Before and since the time of Christ — four of whose disciples were fishermen — men who have gone to sea to feed their families have always been enshrined in the heart of folklore and social history. Theirs was a battle with nature even more hazardous than that of their compatriots farming the land. Lives were forfeit for their livelihood even more often, their families accepting grief with the traditional fortitude of seafaring folk. While the men braved the seas in all weathers in small craft, their women toiled drying, salting, smoking and marketing the fish, keeping the home fires burning literally for their families. The fisherman is surely our greatest folk hero; unsung, he just did his job with valour as he does today in his dedicated rescues from our shores.

Sea angling fish from our coastline today include: bass, mullet, mackerel, pollack, whiting, tope, bream, shark, cod, herring, plaice, flounder, dogfish, sole, conger, ray, skate and turbot.

So much has already been written about fishing in Cornwall that considerations of limited space demand that we confine ourselves to the various tastes and customs concerning the preparation and cooking of only some of these fish, past and present; with particular interest in the past.

Personally, my interest in the subject is heightened because, according to parish records, a direct ancestor, Martin Stodden, was drowned in 1650 while fishing for pilchards in Gerrans Bay — whose waters splash against the seawall near my back door. My maiden name 'Stodden', I have been told, is actually the oldest in the village of Portscatho.

The Pilchard Story

Pilchards and mackerel dominate the history of fish exporting and home consumption in our peninsula. As is told in the opening of this book 'fairmades' (*furmades*) or cured pilchards, became part of the spoken word and continued through centuries as a staple food whether freshly soused (marinated) salted or smoked.

Cornish fishermen used to say that the pilchard was the least in size, the most in number and the greatest for gain of all fish taken from the sea. The big centres of the pilchard fishery of the last century were Mount's Bay, St Ives, and Mevagissey, the last a few miles from my home in Portscatho. The fish were caught primarily by seining and secondly by drift nets.

The procedure after the hauls was invariably the same. The fish were offloaded in the salt cellars or 'palaces' — often beneath the fisherman's dwellings — and left piled with salt between the layers. About a month afterwards they were washed and cleaned and packed into hogsheads, each containing about three thousand fish. After pressing, this oiliest of fish produced about three gallons of oil per barrel if taken in summer and less later, but, what is noteworthy, the fish after extraction of the oil still contained a residue. Probably this was the reason for the popularity of the salted pilchards which (like Cornwall's tin and china clay) became an important export, especially to Italy where it was kept in its strongly salted condition for up to a year. Still remembered is that irreverent toast:

Here's a health to the Pope, may he live to repent
And add half the year to the time of his Lent
To teach all his children from Rome to the Poles
There's nothing like pilchards for saving their souls.

Understandably, since the big pilchard shoals mysteriously left our shores after the turn of the century, some modern booklets on fishing today do not even mention them. Although good catches are still made sometimes, a wholesaler told me there is no price for pilchards. Yet pilchard oil is still in some demand, sold by the litre and tourist fishermen buy it at our local post office in small quantities to preserve hooks and soak their bait.

And yet again, pilchards cured by a Newlyn firm are still exported to Italy where there is a steady if limited demand for them; the manager told me this was a far cry from the six thousand tons exported into Italy to the great grandsire of the original firm there today! Actually I could hardly believe my eyes when I saw three men and five women at the Newlyn curing factory carrying out basically the old brine curing methods (granted, up-dated in some stages of the process) and learnt they were the last people in Britain to be employed thus. Dried fish was also being prepared for export to Italy.

The pilchard story is by no means finished. At Long Rock, Newlyn, freezing and cold store additions to Shippam Ltd were built in 1981, which I was told are capable of processing 45 tons of pilchards a day.

People still refer colourfully to the pilchards they seldom eat now (except in cans) as fairmaids, gipsy herrings and Mevagissey ducks. As observed before, the fairmaid is derived from the Spanish *fumade*, smoked, and gipsy herrings earned their name because they were laid out on the turf to dry before being salted and shipped. As for the expression Mevagissey ducks used by the Royal Navy, my guess is that some sailor-cook acquainted with the small dried fish called Bombay duck in the East, an accompaniment for Indian curries, saw some similarity in salted pilchards.

The pilchard story is interwoven with our past: from the oil (train) used in the little egg-cup-shaped earthenware lamp (the chill or chilla) that stank out every cottage with its smeech, to the salt problems that gave rise to starvation, emigration, smuggling and other malpractices, some of which I have written about for inclusion in a further book. Suffice it to say here that when salt from the valued Breton pans couldn't be imported due to war and English-mined salt was excluded by high taxes, we did have our own sea-evaporation places. The name Salt Ponds near Mousehole bears witness to this.

It is a significant fact that the weight of salt could be higher than that of the weight of the fish or other animal to be cured. An example given at the time of the Napoleonic wars was that it took practically the value of one side of the carcass of a pig to procure enough salt to preserve the other. There were times when pilchard surpluses were sold for manure at 6d per 100, and just because people could not afford the salt tax!

The old ways of preserving pilchards, as other fish caught in the summer season to store for the winter months, comprised chimney smoking, salting and marinating. Salted pilchards, stored in a bussa (earthenware jar), were extracted as required daily and after the salt had been washed out were used for cooking in the crock above the fire or in the oven. By studying the following recipes it is obvious that costly salting was avoided in olden times by cooking the fresh fish in the marinade. Particularly notice Shirley's grandmother's way with mackerel further on. But first of all here are old recipes contributed by members of Perranporth, Truro, and Gerrans and Portscatho WIs included in *Cornish Recipes Ancient and Modern*, compiled by Edith Martin and issued by the Cornwall Federation of Women's Institutes (1929).

How to Salt Pilchards

Get a bussa (earthenware stain) or pan. Place the fish in layers after cleaning, filling the insides with salt, and sprinkle salt thinly on each layer. Cover with a piece of old flannel. Put a stone on top.

Soused (Marinated) Pilchards

Thoroughly clean and wash as many pilchards as will fill an earthenware jar or pan. Put a bay leaf inside each fish and season well with pepper and salt. When the pan is full of fish, pour in sufficient vinegar to cover them, tie down with brown paper and put into a slow oven. Leave all night. It is usual to put this into an oven after the baking is finished, and if the bones of fish are dissolved by next morning, it is ready to serve. If not, return to oven until done. Must be eaten cold.

Scrowled Pilchard

Clean fish and split quite open, mix teaspoonful salt, sugar and pepper, sprinkle well over them, and then 'scrowl' on gridiron over a clear fire.

Pilchards were often chopped up with raw onion and salt and eaten with fingers. A Newlyn source quotes the saying 'fish for fingers, prongs (forks) for mait'. Another old warning: 'Pilchards must be eaten from tail to head.'

Canned Pilchards

At the time of writing, C Shippam Ltd are canning increasing quantities of mackerel and pilchards; mostly for the home market. This fish, canned in Newlyn, is considered to be of superior quality to imported brands.

Many economical, nutritious and tasty meals may be made from canned pilchards. They go further than sardines on toast and mashed with their own tomato sauces are beloved by children for sandwiches. Here, however, the tin of pilchards stretches for a family meal with this hot favourite:

Pilchard Hot Pot

> 4 potatoes, 1 small onion, 1 pinch mixed herbs, salt and pepper, 1 can pilchards in tomato sauce 454 g, 1 small cooking apple, dripping.

Grease a pie dish and line it with very thinly sliced raw potatoes. Turn the pilchards on to this lining together with the sauce. Sprinkle with the onion and apple, minced and mixed. Season with the pepper and herbs and cover with a further layer of sliced potatoes. Brush over with melted dripping, sprinkle lightly with salt and bake at 200°C (400°F) for 30—35 minutes.

How Mackerel Was Kept

For Six Months

Shirley Green tells me that she remembers being told how her grandmother marinated mackerel in large bussas, taking them down to the local bake house to cook slowly overnight in the embers of the fire. The mackerel were cleaned, heads and tails removed, and placed one on top of the other in the bussa. Peppercorns and bay leaves were placed between the layers. A mixture of ⅔ malt vinegar to ⅓ water was then poured over the mackerel. These were then cooked in a very low oven overnight and left to go cold. When cold a layer of fat would appear on the top of the fish, sealing it. Covered down tightly with brown paper or the like, these fish would then last undisturbed for up to six months, or could be dipped into as required.

'I marinated some mackerel myself a few years back in August and when opened in January they were still edible and much enjoyed,' says Shirley.

Mackerel is best grilled or baked in the oven, whole or filleted.

Mackerel with Gooseberry Sauce

Very Cornish is this gourmet dish. As usual for grilling or frying, slit the fish down the belly and remove the backbone. Season, fold over, dry and fry in hardly any fat, or grill. Pour over the following sauce, reserving more to serve separately.

The classic gooseberry sauce for serving with mackerel was made from wild gooseberries, but cultivated fruit is as good. Top and tail about 250 g (½ lb) of berries and stew in hardly any water until they are soft and pulpy. Beat well and then pass through a sieve or purée them in a blender. Depending on the age of the fruit, add a little sugar. Mix in 25 g (1 oz) butter.

Mackerel with Cider and Rhubarb

Rhubarb is as effective a sauce as are gooseberries with mackerel, cutting the oiliness. Each of 8 fillets of fish is rolled up with a bay leaf and peppercorn inside, covered with cider and dotted with butter, then baked in a moderate oven for ½ hour.

For the Rhubarb Sauce: About 450 g (1 lb) rhubarb, 4 tablespoons brown sugar, a few drops of lemon juice, ½ teaspoon nutmeg and 8 tablespoons of cider are simmered until the rhubarb becomes a fairly dry purée. Serve sieved or as it is in a sauceboat with the mackerel.

Smoked Mackerel

Mackerel should be eaten day-fresh and cannot be frozen. That is why it is popular smoked. Those who smoke their own fish please note that it is preferably smoked in one piece and not in fillets. Smoke boxes are obtainable at a few specialist shops (one is in Falmouth). The smoking of meats is not an expensive art and a fisherman particularly enjoys smoking his catch. The flavour of the smoking depends on the sawdust used; this should be of hard wood such as oak, and is obtainable from sawmills here.

Smoked Mackerel Pâté

(a) 2 smoked mackerel*, 250 g (½ lb) butter, 150 ml (¼ pint) cream, juice of 1 lemon, salt and black pepper freshly ground.

*(Charlestown smokeries produce the best we have tasted so far.)

Skin and bone the fish. Melt butter gently, beat or liquidise with the mackerel flesh, then add cream, lemon juice and seasoning.

(b)   450 g (1 lb) smoked mackerel fillets, 250 g (½ lb) smooth cottage cheese, tabasco sauce, salt and pepper, juice of 2 lemons.

Marinate the fish in the lemon juice for three hours. Skin the fillets, blend until smooth with the other ingredients. Chill, sprinkle with paprika and serve on fingers of toast.

NB: If unable to buy the smooth (homogenised) cottage cheese in cartons remember some supermarkets sell it in bulk. For example, at time of writing, I obtain mine from International Stores.

Fisherman Cooks His Catch
This Easy Way

Easiest way to cook fish is the fisherman's way: Catch it yourself, clean and wrap, without scaling, in a wet brown paper or even a newspaper; place the bundle among the hot embers of the fire on the beach or at home in the oven. When the paper starts to peel and brown the bundle is unrolled and the scales will be found adhering to the paper. Under the skin is delicately cooked white flesh.

Supplementing the mackerel and pilchards in the daily fish diet of our coastal ancestors were salted cod, ling and numerous other fish. But they were all, generally speaking, prepared in a similar way. Namely soaked overnight to extract the salt, simmered until tender with herbs on the slab (stove) and served with a mustard or other piquant sauce to tart up the dish.

A Sauce for Smoked and Salted Fish

Beat the yolks of 2 eggs and mix them with ½ cup softened butter and a tablespoon lemon juice. Put into the top of a double saucepan or into a heat proof pot set in a small saucepan of hot water. Over a slow heat, beat the sauce continuously until it thickens; if required add a little water to make it the consistency of thick cream. Season and serve over de-salted fish. Mustard may be added.

Salt Cod with Parsnips

This was a traditional Lenten dish for Ash Wednesday served with egg sauce and enjoyed by old-timers to this day. The salted fish, as usual, was de-salted by leaving for 12 hours or so in water and changing the water twice if the fish was very salt. It was then cooked in water below the boil (to ensure it didn't harden) and, barely simmering, left on the lowest heat for about 20 minutes. The fish was then drained and served whole on a napkin accompanied by mashed turnips (Cornish for 'swedes') and egg sauce.

Bass

This delicately-fleshed fish should be fried or poached and the sauce should never overwhelm its flavour. Bass is also delicious and very filling when stuffed and baked (see recipe for Conger Eel).

Fillets of Sole

Grilling is the easiest and most gratifying of the hundreds of ways you can prepare sole. Flatten skinned fillets slightly, season, brush with oil or melted butter and cook under a moderate grill. Serve hot garnished with parsley and lemon segments. Choice accompaniments for sole are asparagus tips or tiny mushrooms in a cream sauce. Fillets poached in a fish fumet or court bouillon and served with a shrimp sauce, or cooked en casserole curled and packed together are further sole successes.

Grey Mullet

This is more abundant than the prized red mullet. Grey mullet is cooked, using the same recipe as bass. It is known as 'leaping fish', French *poisson sauteur*.

Red Mullet

At my brother-in-law's hotel at Soar Mill Cove in Devon I tasted red mullet grilled to perfection. My sister, Norma, being a Cornish woman, qualifies for her recipe in this Cornish book. She points out that this tender fish should be handled carefully. Because fishermen traditionally leave in the gut, red mullet should be cooked right away untrimmed. Some connoisseurs do not even gut it or remove the scales, just butter it and grill under a low heat to be served with parsley and lemon. But Norma's way 'to present the mullet looking alive and retaining its full red colour,' is as follows:

Gut and clean the fish by slitting the underbelly and cleansing the cavity with gently running water. After lightly salting the interior, rub a mixture of crushed almonds (crushed in the same way as garlic) and lemon juice with a little oreganum and/or other herbs. Lay the fish on a buttered glass dish. Glaze lightly with lemon-butter and cook in a microwave oven for 3½ minutes at 600 watts, turning half time and glazing lightly again. Take out and glaze very lightly once more, sprinkle the top with grated almonds and grill for one minute under the ordinary oven grill.

Whiting

Including a Breton Way

I grill my fish brushed with oil for health considerations, but whiting is excellent dipped in milk and flour and fried. Just before serving, sprinkle with lemon juice and a little pepper and salt. A Breton way with whiting is as follows: Make a shallow incision along the back of the fish. Season and place in a buttered heatproof dish. Pour over a few dessertspoons of dry white wine and a little lemon juice. Bring gently to the boil on top of the stove then finish in a moderate oven until the fish is tender, basting with lemon juice. (And when using lemon or tomatoes please remember those few grains of sugar.)

Conger Eel Recipes

With Cider and Stuffed

Although some people refused to eat conger eel, many families did rely on many meals from just one fish (and there is an increasing demand for 'conger' today). Top and tail went into stew and the middle part was fried in lard or boiled with leeks and parsley. One traditional recipe, stuffed and baked, goes as follows:

Take a piece from the middle part of a large conger eel, about 12″ in length, clean it without opening, stuff with a forecemeat made of seasoned breadcrumbs, shredded suet, parsley and thyme, securing both ends with a larded paper. Dredge the fish with flour and bake it in the oven and baste it regularly. Add a tumblerful of cider to the pan and continue basting. Turn when half done. Tomato sauce was a favourite with baked eel.

Shark

The exciting shark fishing off Looe has invested shark with eating glamour and several dishes are made from it. It is sometimes cut into small chunks when finished to simulate Lobster Thermidor. Most prized of all shark meat is that of the polbeagle, usually fished on the North coasts.

Skate or Ray?

Prepared the Same Way

When I marvelled at the huge winged fish being off-loaded by a trawler at Padstow Harbour and referred to them as skate, the manager of the fish market on the quay corrected me, 'We sell them as rays,' he said. He was too busy for me to pursue the subject further but, as I later learned, the large ray family is an enterprising group in evolution. Some fly through the water instead of swimming and the thornback ray (roker) produces those roe bags known as 'mermaids purses', a common sight in the jetsam of the beach; but not to be confused with the smaller purses of the dog fish. Another ray, the 'eagle', a large stinging type, dispenses with roe and purses and actually gives birth to its young alive, as do some sharks.

The flesh of skate and ray are white and meaty, but not oily. As cartilage replaces bone in the skate, the whole fish is prized by the French who use the gelatinous cuttings and cartilage for soup, fish stock and sauces for other fish.

Here in Cornwall only the wings of the skate are used and the body dumped, except in the case of some exported to France (which takes 70% of our local catches) where sometimes the whole fish is used, including the liver which is considered a delicacy and is served with the wings or made into fritters or pâté.

Wings of Skate

Traditional

Wash wings well and hang up for 24 hours to drain and mature. Then simmer gently in salted water to cover the fish. When the fish starts to separate from the cartilage (gelatinous muscle in the case of the skate, **not** bones), drain and serve with caper sauce, hot or cold. Nasturtium seeds make a mock caper sauce (see Index).

The Tasty Liver: (1) Simmer the liver until tender then chop up with parsley. (2) Or dip into lemon juice and oil then fry. (3) Or make fritters from the liver by poaching pieces in white wine or dry cider. Then marinate in oil, lemon juice or dry cider and salt and pepper. Just before serving, drain and dry and dip into a light batter and fry in very hot oil. Season with salt and garnish with fried parsley and lemon.

Fried Skate

Small fish are used whole for this in France but here the wings are bought already skinned, in keeping with our tradition. To fry, cut in chunks or use in wing form, according to the size of the fish. Soak the fish in cold boiled milk, drain and lightly flour each piece then plunge into hot fat. Season and serve as given for the liver above.

Caper sauce is a favourite with skate but melted butter, parsley, onion, shrimp and anchovy sauces are featured with skate on menus.

Tip for 'boning' skate: After simmering the wings until flesh is tender and just about to part from the 'bones', lift out and drain the wings. Holding the wing flat with a cloth wrung out in cold water, the bones may be drawn out sideways — all of a piece.

Fish Roes

Roes are sold in such quantity at fishmongers in Cornwall, the presumption is that the taste for them has survived the past when all of the fish was important food.

Roes for Croquettes

680 g (1½ lb) fish roe, cleaned, washed, and cooked in salted water, 3 tablespoons butter, ⅓ cup flour, 1¼ cup milk (scalded), salt and pepper, 1 egg (beaten), breadcrumbs, ½ teaspoon Worcestershire sauce, ½ teaspoon grated onion.

Prepare a white sauce with butter, flour and milk. Add salt, pepper, onion and sauce. Break up the cooked fish roe, omit skin and fold into sauce. Chill thoroughly. Form into croquettes. Dip in beaten egg, then in breadcrumbs and fry in hot oil until brown.

Roes in Milk

450 g (1 lb) fish roes, milk, salt and pepper, 1 tablespoon cornflour, butter, chopped parsley.

Wash roes, removing loose skin. Simmer in sufficient milk to cover. Season with salt and pepper. Drain roes when cooked and thicken milk with cornflour, mixed to a paste with a little cold water. Stir until sauce is smooth. Just before serving add butter and parsley.

To Pickle Sprats

A Recipe of 1698

Take a peck of the largest sprats, without heads, and salt them a little overnight; then take a pot or barrel and lay in it a layer of Bay salt; and then some sprats, and a few Bay leaves with a little lemon peel. Thus do till you have filled the vessel, then cover and pitch it that no air get in, set it in a cool cellar, and once in a week turn it upside down; in three months you may eat them.

Fried Fish in Batter

3 tablespoons flour, 1 tablespoon cornflour, salt and pepper, monosodium glutamate, ½ cup warm water, 1 tablespoon melted butter, 1 egg, separated, and cooked or raw fish.

Stir water, butter and egg yolk into sifted dry ingredients. Fold in stiffly beaten egg white. Add fish, well dried and not greasy. Drop into very hot oil, reduce heat and when cooked, remove and drain on absorbent paper. Keep warm. Garnish with parsley and lemon wedges.

Fish Sticks with Lemon Butter

Today's 'Make Do'

In tribute to our frozen fish products there is much we can do on a small outlay. Consider fish sticks and forget about the deep oil cooking; remember we cook better with a **shortage** of oil. To serve two or three:

1 package of frozen fish sticks, grated Parmesan cheese, or any cheese on hand, 3 tablespoons butter or margarine, 1 tablespoon lemon juice, 2 teaspoons capers.

Sprinkle fish sticks with cheese and bake according to package directions. Melt butter and add lemon juice and capers. Spoon this sauce on to the fish sticks.

Poor Man's Scampi

Using Monkfish

Scampi is supposedly Dublin Bay prawns but when commercially deep frozen for you to fry **may** include other mollusc bodies. When you cut up the tail of monkfish and fry it for a mock scampi at least you know exactly what you are cooking.

Skin and fillet out the large centre bone. Cut the thick flesh into approximately 1½" cubes, coat in egg and breadcrumbs and fry in the usual way.

NB: Monkfish, known as angel shark in other counties, is known in Cornwall as the angler fish (Hophius piscatorius).

Mock Crab Cocktail

Monkfish Again

450 g (1 lb) monkfish fillets, fresh or frozen, ½ teaspoon salt, ½ medium sized onion, sliced.

Simmer the fillets of fish in salted water with the onion for 20 minutes until the fish is tender but quite firm. Cut the drained fish into ½" pieces and chill.

For the Sauce: ½ cup mayonnaise, ½ tablespoon lemon juice, 3 tablespoons tomato sauce, 1 teaspoon chopped parsley, ½ teaspoon finely chopped onion, ⅛ teaspoon tabasco, ¼ teaspoon anchovy essence (optional). Serves 4.

Combine mayonnaise, lemon juice, tomato sauce, parsley, onion, tabasco and anchovy essence. Fold this into the chilled fish pieces on a bed of shredded lettuce. Decorate with tomato, slice of egg and a sprig of parsley, according to whether you are serving this in individual glass bowls or as a centrepiece dish.

Haddock and Kippers

Kippers — 'No Smell'

Loved for breakfast and farmhouse teas are the haddock and kipper. Everyone knows that you put the haddock on the pan in cold water and go on changing the water until the acrid taste is drowned away, then finish in milk and water, seasoned as desired. But not everyone may know about the latest way to cook kipper, saving the smell that always accompanies its cooking. A London chef, Richard Schnyder, says it is easy to prepare an odourless kipper: Lightly beat an egg, add salt and pepper, then coat each kipper fillet with a thin layer of beaten egg and lightly fry in butter in the same manner as *meuniere*. All the taste, no smell!

What is Whitebait?

These small fried fish may be a combination of smelts, eel, sprats, herring or any other small species of fish.

FISH FROM OUR RIVERS

The Tamar and Fowey rivers and hundreds of streams in our peninsula have always been rich in freshwater fisheries. Determined by poaching regulations through the ages, salmon, trout and lamprey have abounded, but only occasionally filling the poor man's stomach. All poaching in the Duchy was severely punished.

Tamar Salmon

Traditional Recipe

Clean and scale the fish, then put the whole salmon into a fish kettle or suitable pot, add cold water almost to cover the fish, then three tablespoons of cooking oil and a little salt and pepper. Bring water gently to the boil. Let it simmer for 5 minutes (no longer). Then leave to cool in its own liquor. Serve cold with new potatoes nicely glazed with butter and cucumber, sliced.

Grilled Tamar Salmon

Season salmon steaks lightly with salt and pepper, brush with olive oil and grill under moderate heat for about 8 minutes, turning a few times while basting with a brushing of oil. Garnish with parsley and lemon. Salmon is sometimes served with lobster, shrimp and anchovy sauce but the fish in itself when cooked at its prime is best served in the old way with its own liquor to which a little fennel and butter may be added.

Trout

Once the delight of a favoured few, trout is now on the menus; the reason being its availability frozen. The simplest way is to fry it.

2 fresh brook trout or one 289 g (10 oz) package of frozen trout, thawed, 2 teaspoons lemon juice, 1 teaspoon salt, 3 tablespoons flour, ⅛ teaspoon pepper, ¼ cup salad oil, 1 medium sliced onion.

Clean and scale trout if necessary. Sprinkle lemon juice and ½ teaspoon salt in cavity. Combine remaining salt, flour and pepper, roll trout in mixture to coat. Slowly heat salad oil in a large frying pan until a drop of water sizzles when added. Sauté trout for 5 minutes or until golden. Turn and sauté other side for 1 minute. Add onion and cook over medium heat about 5 minutes or until fish is nicely browned.

Fresh Trout

Coat the fresh trout in seasoned flour, melt 1 tablespoon butter and a little oil in the frying pan and fry over moderate heat as above. Lay trout on hot serving platter. To serve, add ½ cup soured cream to sediment in frying pan then pour at once over the fish. Almonds blanched and fried in butter may be added for garnishing. Serve with small boiled potatoes and asparagus.

Salmon Trout

Appearing on the menu as Salmon Trout this delicate, delicious fish is actually one of seven sea-going trout and its characteristic pink flesh seems to depend on its food crustacea. Talking to Mr Richard Harris who supplies this type of trout to leading hotels and restaurants throughout Britain, I happened on yet another success story for our county. My visit to the unique hatchery of *Fowey Sea Products Ltd*, which is amazing its competitors by producing sea-going (salt water) trout to full size at one-third of the time taken at other sea farms, just begs to be told here; but lack of space indicates the priority of the recipe.

To my mind a light grilling with a soupcon of lemon juice and seasoning is the only way to present this delectable fish. Yet for those who must dress it up cordon bleu here is a recipe with wine.

675 g (1½ lb) salmon trout, 2 wineglasses of white wine, 1 wine-glass of water — to make 300 ml (½ pint) liquid, a squeeze of lemon juice, salt, pepper, bouquet garni, 1 shallot (chopped), 25 g (1 oz) butter, 3 egg yolks, 3 tablespoons double cream, 38g (1½ oz) unsalted butter, 1 cucumber.

Wash, dry and trim the trout, place in a shallow dish with the wine, water and seasoning. Cover and bring to simmering point gently, then leave to poach for 20 minutes. Drain fish and reserve the liquor. Fry the chopped shallot in butter until just golden, then pour over the fish liquor and reduce it by cooking until half the amount. Now make the sauce. Thicken the liquid with the egg yolks and cream stirring continuously over lowest heat, then beat in the unsalted butter, bit by bit. Pass through a strainer. The cucumber is cooked after peeling and quartered lengthways then fried until just tender. To serve: Skin the fish, spoon the sauce over it and serve hot surrounded by the cucumber.

Lamprey

Lamprey is an eel-like fresh water vertebrate fish and has been eaten since ancient times. It was usually hung some time to mature before cooking. It was cooked like conger but took twice as long to soften. As Henry 1st died from a 'surfeit of lamprey' we presume he must have had it richly stuffed with an unholy forcemeat of herbs and cured pork. For Cornish labourers it was a treat merely stewed for hours on the open hearth with barley dumplings.

Fish à l'Armoricaine

For Any White Freshwater Fish

Original Breton dishes are known by the appellations à la Cancalaise, à la Nantaise, à la Bretonne and, most importantly, à l'Armoricaine. Armorica, of course, was the name before we Britons started our first colony there, at the time of the saints, reminding us yet again, it was many years later before we came to be known as Cornwall. An understandable error on a menu is to confuse Armoricaine with American. However, fortunately, in these parts we do 'know our onions'; although the following fish dish uses garlic and shallots instead.

> 1 white freshwater fish about 1·5 kg (3 lb) after cleaning and boning, 2 cloves garlic, 2 shallots, 4 tablespoons olive oil, 3 oz (75 g) flour, ½ bottle dry white wine, 5 large tomatoes, 2 teaspoons sugar, 1 tablespoon tomato paste, bouquet garni, salt, pepper, 2½ oz (70 g) butter, 4 tablespoons single cream or top of milk, cayenne pepper, 2 tablespoons chopped parsley. Cognac for flaming if desired.

Chop the garlic and shallots fairly finely. On a low heat cook them in 1 tablespoon olive oil, stirring all the time. Cut the boned fish into six pieces (for serving six). Sprinkle with flour and brown lightly in olive oil in a separate pan. Drain from oil and moisten with cognac and flame. After which add the wine, bouquet garni, and the seeded tomatoes, peeled and chopped. Add the sugar and the tomato paste. Season, cover and allow to simmer for 25 minutes. Remove the fish from the pan and put aside to keep hot. Remove the bunch of bouquet garni from the liquid in the pan and add the butter mixed with flour for a roux for thickening, stirring all the time. Simmer the sauce for a few minutes. Remove from heat to stir in cream or top of milk, add a little cayenne then re-heat with the fish. Serve garnished with parsley.

Court Bouillon for Poaching Fish

55 g (2 oz) carrots, 55 g (2 oz) onion, 2 white peppercorns, pinch of salt, 142 ml (¼ pint) wine vinegar or white wine, 840 ml (1½ pints) water, 1 bouquet garni.

Slice the vegetables finely and place in a pan with the water, the bouquet garni and the peppercorns. Bring to the boil, skim and simmer until the vegetables are tender. Strain and add the vinegar.

The Future of Fish

Low in cholesterol, fish in all its exciting variety of species, is the best of all health proteins. It now remains for us, the consumers, to learn more about its cooking and presentation so that restaurant patrons and our families will create the demand for it. It also remains for fish mongers to bring the prices of fish down to compete with poultry and the cheaper meats.

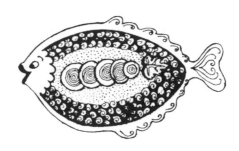

MOLLUSCS AND CRUSTACEA

Returning after 50 years in South Africa with its thousands of miles of mollusc and crustacea rich coastline, it seems incredible to me that here in Cornwall with our mere 245 miles you can go to the beach collecting winkles and mussels **free**. My cousin Nancy goes winkling and prawning with never a glance over her shoulder for a police car or helicopter. Who worries if she has more than 50 prawns or winkles in her bag? The seagull there (and here) may be seen at that dramatic game of swooping out of the sky to seize a mussel, then carrying it aloft, dropping it to crack open on the rocks below, followed by its spectacular sky-dive *coup de grace*. Yet while the South African gulls can do it, any **person** taking more than 25 black mussels, 50 white mussels or 50 periwinkles from the Government-controlled coastline is subject to the equivalent of a £3000 fine or five years, or both. And it is so often the poor coloured fisherman seeking bait who gets caught. No wonder Britain is still idolised by the underprivileged of other countries, with so much here still for free — conservation-conscious as we are.

Trigging or trygging, the gathering of shellfish, was traditional here in Cornwall on Good Fridays, a time when the tides are exceptionally low, favourite trygging spots being Par sands and Helford River where the old custom survives to this day. Among the univalves or gastropods are the following.

Cockles

Cardium Edule

Fried with bacon cockles can be a treat, if you known how to dig for them. Like other shellfish, they should be cleaned and left in a bucket of fresh water overnight, then boiled for five minutes, then fried.

Winkles

Periwinkles or winkles, also called sea-snails locally, require the art of the 'pin and the twist' and you need half a dozen for a real mouthful, raw. Or soak them with an escape-proof lid on top of the bucket and cook by simmering for ten minutes after plunging them into boiling water.

Limpets

We are warned not to collect from piers or jetties, but somewhere safely washed by the tides. A knife or a kick with the foot can loosen them from the rocks. When collected, wash off all sand and put in a saucepan with cold water, then bring to the boil and boil until they slip out of their shells. Serve cold with wine vinegar and freshly ground black pepper.

Clams

Bivalves

This mussel-like shellfish is sometimes found when digging for cockles. The name can be confusing as scallops and large cockles are sometimes referred to as clams. They take longer to cook than other shellfish. After scalding in boiling water for 10 minutes the fish is removed from the shell and fried, baked or boiled, as required. The American 'clambakes' as well as the clam chowder soups are famous. Nearer home our Breton cousins use them extensively, Roscoff being a centre of the clam trade.

Mussels

Here is one of the most popular of shellfish. Be aware of any publicity concerning the 'red tide' (toxic plankton) and follow the tests for collecting shellfish.

Check for shellfish: Always gather them in healthy spots, not close to houses or anywhere sewage may be pumped into the sea. Always leave them to cleanse in frequent changes of tap water for some hours. Always wash them well, insides as well as outsides in clean water. Check that a shellfish is alive before cooking. This is done by forcing an opening of the shell, then reducing pressure. If the shell fails to close again it may be assumed it is dead.

Similarly with oysters, mussels may be eaten raw but are better cooked, as the flesh is tougher than that of the oyster. Clean, then steam until they are open, drain and remove from shells. Put 2 mussels into each half shell. When cool mix 4 tablespoons butter, 1 crushed clove of garlic, salt and pepper and 1 dessertspoon chopped parsley. Spread mussels with this savoury butter, dust with fine breadcrumbs and bake at 230°C (450°F) for 10 minutes. Brown under grill if necessary and serve hot with thin slices of wholewheat or rye bread and butter.

Mussels à la Mariniere

With Frozen Mussels

Wash 4 dozen mussels in several waters. Put the mussels into a pan with 2 small onions, chopped parsley or other herbs, chopped chives and a cup of white wine and a tablespoon butter. Simmer with lid on for about 15 minutes until shells open of their own accord. Take out the onions. Pass all through a colander retaining the mussels and use the juice they were cooked in as a sauce.

Mussel and Spinach Sandwich

For Today

This open sandwich consists of strips of puréed spinach, mussels and scrambled egg. The mussels, alive and washed, are cooked in their shells by placing them in a pan without water over heat for 5 minutes. With the shells removed, they are arranged in a strip down the middle of a slice of buttered brown bread, flanked by a strip of scrambled egg and puréed spinach.

Oysters

The healthier the oyster the more difficult the shell is to open. When a shell opens immediately on touching the fish is unfit to eat. Before presenting an oyster party I get a strong man wearing leather gloves to prise the oysters from their shells. Each arranged on its deep shell, all rest on a sea of green seaweed or parsley on trays covered with kitchen foil interspersed with segments of lemon. The only accompaniment is brown bread and butter. In line with purists the world over who swallow the fish neat at one gulp pepper need not be supplied, although some do enjoy cayenne.

We Cornish loved adding any available oysters to a stew or meat pie, legitimately bought or occasionally in the past poached from the prolific oyster beds at the mouth of the Helford, Fal and Percuil rivers. The sad story of the disease that has spread from Brittany to our natural oyster beds here has been bad for business. But the fact remains that Brittany has suffered the same disease for many years without harm to those who eat their oysters, convincing us that publicity can harm us more than the actual disease; in this oyster case, at least.

Cooked oysters are used for sauces, soups, and stuffings, in a pilau with chicken and other meats, or curried and devilled, made into fritters and omelettes and smoked for hors d'oeuvre or cocktail snacks. These are now available reasonably priced in tins. From scores of recipes we select the simplest ones.

Baked Oysters

Place each oyster in its deep half shell. Line a baking sheet with cooking salt. Squeeze a few drops of lemon juice on each oyster and season with a sprinkling of cayenne pepper. Sprinkle with fried breadcrumbs then pour over some melted butter seasoned with lemon, salt and pepper. Brown in a very hot oven. Serve on a napkin garnished with fresh parsley.

Oysters à la Florentine

Fill the deep halves of the oyster shells with a layer of spinach puréed with butter. Put a raw oyster on top of each one. Cover with creamy cheese sauce, sprinkle with grated cheese and brown in oven.

Oysters in Sherry Cream

Heat a shallow casserole and in the meantime bring 1 cup of cream to boiling point, then add ½ cup sherry. Pour the sherry and cream mixture into a warm casserole and add about a litre (1 quart) of well-drained fresh oysters. Spread them out evenly and season well with salt and pepper, then cover with well-buttered breadcrumbs. Place under the grill just long enough to brown the breadcrumbs and heat up the oysters until they curl at the edges. Serve with toast and green salad and a semi-dry white wine or cider.

Creamed Oysters on Toast

Simmer about ½ litre (1 pint) oysters in their own liquid over a very low heat for 10 minutes or until edges curl and oysters are plump. Drain. Melt 1 tablespoon butter in a frying pan, then blend in 1 tablespoon flour and stir their broth in gradually. Cook and stir until thickened. Fold in a cup of light cream and heat. Add a little hot sauce to 4 beaten egg yolks, then return this to the hot mixture.

Stir over low heat until thickened. Add oysters and heat thoroughly. Stir in 2 teaspoons lemon juice and sprinkle with parsley. Serve on points of toast.

One or Two Oysters?

Serve on skewers, alternated with cubes of fried brown bread and mushrooms. The pieces of oyster can be dipped in lemon juice and grilled lightly, seasoned with black pepper.

The Mighty Scallop

The scallop was used as a fertility symbol and by seafarers in the East long before the Phoenicians traded for our alluvial tin at Mount Ictis. It was also the badge of pilgrimage fixed to mantle and hat of the pilgrims crossing from Wales to be joined by our own Cornish pilgrims from Padstow to Fowey, then via Mont-St-Michel in Brittany to their destination, the shrine of St James at Compostela in north western Spain. I have never been sure if they earned their scallops when they got there or flaunted them before. Some historian please tell me!

The scallop, of course, inspired Boticelli to paint *The Birth of Venus* (Aphrodite — 1478) and we are not surprised when tasting this delicate shellfish, unspoilt by too strong a sauce. The shell is indeed a thing of beauty and the flesh divine. They may be eaten raw with lemon juice in the same way as oysters.

My cousin Nancy suggests that some people boil scallops too hard and too long. To play safe and to be sure they are tender she **simmers** her scallops for no longer than five minutes, then dresses them with a light lemon or cheese sauce incorporating the liquid they were poached in.

Scallops, fresh and alive, are sold on occasions locally. To open Nancy puts them in the oven at a very low heat, the rounded part downwards. They soon open completely. The flesh and the coral are poached in a court-bouillon made with white wine, seasoned and with a little onion, thyme and bayleaf. They can then be used in many ways including mayonnaise for hors d'oeuvre, or fried and threaded kebab fashion with other seafood. The few I can afford I pass through flour and cook with bacon, turning with the spatula as required.

Large scallop shells have been used from the beginning of time for cooking and serving ware and even now some farmwives find them useful in the dairy for skimming clouted cream.

Scallops à la Nantaise

This Breton dish is from that beautifully illustrated book *The Living Scallop* by 8 authors (Shell Transport and Trading Company 1957). It is suggested it be washed down with a fairly sweet cider.

Obtain good shellfish, remove the flesh and discard the black portions. Take two receptacles. In one place the white part and the roe, in the other the beards. Press the beards hard so as to extract the moisture, and slice them. Meanwhile melt some butter slowly in a saucepan with two minced onions, mix the hashed beards in with a wooden spoon and leave to simmer with a bouquet garni of herbs and a clove of garlic for a good half hour. While this is cooking, cut the white parts into slices and place them in the preparation to cook slowly for a quarter of an hour. Take off the fire, add some crumbs of bread, butter, and a heaped tablespoon of fresh-pounded parsley. Butter the empty shells, fill them three-quarters full and on each one put a piece of roe, a little grated bread-crumbs, and a piece of butter. Return to a very hot oven for five minutes and serve in the shells.

Queens

Not Little Scallops

Queens, those diminutive-looking scallops are not the same species. Turning the pages of that fine book *The Scallop* already referred to, the beautifully produced old paintings indicate that while the large scallop was applied to the gown or mantle, the 'queen' graced the hat or headgear of pilgrims and others before them, who cherished the shells for their decorative design; in the same way architects have used the design for shell niches and in other parts of buildings from Roman times.

The Queen (*Chlamys opercularis*), 'closheens' in Ireland, is eaten with relish by those with winkling patience. Shirley extends her motherly patience to her shellfish-loving family when she cooks queens. One needs plenty of time and the 'patience of Job' for this recipe, but it is well worth-while just for the flavour. There needs to be at least a couple of dozen queens per person as the white meat is only the size of a thumb nail when extracted.

Open the queens by inserting a knife between the shells, extract the white meat from the centre (the only part Shirley uses). rinse in water. drain and place in a casserole sprinkled with pepper and dot with knobs of butter. Place in a medium hot oven for about 30 minutes, turning the meat after about 15 minutes. Serve with a sprinkling of vinegar and plenty of bread and butter.

Crustacea

While cockles and mussels were used by the majority of working people, the crabs, lobsters and crawfish graced the tables of the farmers and gentry and, packed alive in seaweed, went up to London markets. These creatures had no value except alive and even today they are frozen alive for supplying restaurants — to be cooked alive. The controversy whether it is kinder to plunge a crab into boiling water or into cold water, bringing it slowly to the boil, might continue through the years if someone had not invented an electrical instrument to stun it before it is boiled. This gadget is not yet on the market but is sure to be by the time this book is. Our postmistress Joan, who dresses crab to perfection, always 'drowns' the crab in fresh (tap) water first before bringing it to the boil in salted water.

Crayfish or Lobster?

Crawfish — if Marine

Strictly speaking a crayfish is a freshwater fish and Breton recipes for *écrivesse* use these small lobster-like crustacea from rivers and streams. The misnomer crayfish for crawfish (the marine counterpart) is common, too, in South Africa, although *Jasus lalundi* — its Latin name in those waters — is exported under the name of 'rock lobster'. This is yet another confusion of names perpetuated by the demands of the menu. For example, how much more inviting is Crayfish Cocktail than Lobster or Crawfish Cocktail?

Yet before the preparation of these creatures by any name you like, smile with me at an old French story told by Elizabeth Lucas in her historic *Pretty Kettle of Fish*. She describes how a complete convent of nuns was excommunicated because of 'the nuns excessive devotion to crayfish ("*écrivisse*") in the cooking of which they delighted more than in the singing of psalms.' Although a bishop was sent to reprimand them, on his second visit he found the convent of Bons barred against him, so Cardinal Richelieu had to intervene and outlawed the Abbess of Bons to a strictly supervised nunnery. As the Abbess had begged the recipe from the prior of an adjacent monastery here is surely the setting for a play featuring male chauvinism à la gourmet! The prior and his monks do not appear to have been reprimanded and were left to enjoy *écrivisse* ad lib, prepared extravagantly with a sauce of 'champagne, white wine,

A convent of nuns was excommunicated.

carrots, garlic, onion and herbs, the rind of an orange, salt and pepper; all of these ingredients having been added to a meat stock, reduced to a thick consistency and poured over 10 dozen crayfish.'

Baked Crawfish

Kill crawfish then place right side up with tail outstretched and halve lengthways with large sharp knife. Remove sack and intestine. Scoop out the green liver and remaining coral roe, place in a mixing bowl and mash until creamy. Add remaining ingredients and mix thoroughly. Place crawfish halves side by side on a baking tray, flesh side up. Spoon half of prepared mixture over the flesh and bake at 180°C (350°F) for 13 minutes for average size crawfish. Spoon remaining mixture over crawfish and place under grill for 4 minutes or until turning golden. Remove crawfish on to a heated serving dish and pour over juices from the pan or serve separately in a sauceboat. Serve immediately with French bread to mop up sauce. Serve with a not-too-sweet cider or white wine.

Lobster may be grilled in a similar way to that used for crab, for example, not traditional Cornish but so often on local hotel menus is the following:

Lobster or Crab Thermidor

Cut boiled lobsters or crabs in half lengthwise. Clean and remove meat, discard thread from the centre of tail and 'dead man's fingers' in the case of crab. Dice and sauté in 2 tablespoons butter for 5 minutes. Stir in 2 tablespoons flour until smooth. Add 1 cup cream or milk and stir until blended. Add seasoning of a teaspoon dry mustard, salt to taste, a tablespoon finely chopped parsley, then stir in ⅓ cup white wine or dry cider. Put mixture in lobster shells, sprinkle with grated cheese and a sprinkling of cayenne. Bake stuffed shells in hot oven 200°C (400°F) for about 10 minutes. Serve hot.

Crabs — Grilled

The adequate description of dressing a crab is beyond the space of this book requiring, as it does, clear illustrations. Villagers have learnt the art from 'mother's knee'. But nothing equals a live demonstration. Your fishmonger, however, will prepare the **cooked** crab you buy from him by opening it up and removing the 'dead man's fingers' as they call them here. White and yellowish as may be, all the rest of the inside is edible. Crack the shell to extract the flesh, pull off and crack the claws and crack off the rim of shell around the main carapace, which is easily done. Mix the flesh with melted butter, salt and pepper, stuff the shell and brush with melted butter, then grill for about 10 minutes. An easy tasty sauce to pour over this consists of the juice of ½ lemon, melted butter and a teaspoon of good curry powder.

Cook the crab in a court bouillon usual for shellfish made from stock (or wine, or water), salt, thyme and bayleaf. When cold garnish with parsley and serve with sauce tartare. The sauce is made by adding mayonnaise to finely chopped shallots or young onions and green herbs such as parsley, chervil and tarragon, etc.

Crabmeat and Cider

Fishmongers sell crab ready dressed, a pulp within a crab shell. I happened upon a place near Mousehole where the flesh is blown mechanically out of the crab and sold by the kilo. This fresh crabmeat is ready to use in many delectable ways from stuffings to fritters, salads to sauces and in scallop shells, suitably dressed. If you ask for a shell as well, the easiest of all ways is to fill the crab shell, pour over some scrumpy to moisten the flesh, grate over the top a little grated mature cheddar cheese and grill lightly.

Spider Crabs

Known in the Portscatho area as 'gabrick' and in St Mawes as Granfer Jenkins', the claw meat is the only part worth eating. In fact old fishermen did not bother even to bring the body ashore — just the claws. The meat is sweeter than other crab meat and still enjoyed when available, by the discerning. These crabs are exported in large quantities to the Channel Islands and France where there is a good market for them.

Prawns or Shrimps?

Not the Same

With mild weather during May and a suitable low tide my cousin Nancy and her friends go prawning. The prawns look so miniature I tease the prawners that they are catching shrimps, and the reply is 'probably small prawns.' Fiction? Not fact? Most Cornish authors refer to prawning (not shrimping) and Lady Vyvyan, for one, in her book *The Helford River* (Peter Owen Ltd) describes the pastime in alluring detail. The prawn and the shrimp, of course, are different species. The edible prawn (*Palaemon serratus*) may be up to four inches long and has a greyish partly transparent body. The edible shrimp (*Crangon vulgaris*) is from one inch to three inches long and resembles the prawn but has only one pair of feelers and instead of the bold projecting rostrum has a very insignificant beak. When cooked the creatures turn pinkish in colour.

Shrimps are widely sold in all supermarkets and fish shops, the former selling them in bulk deep frozen. Prawn sandwiches, cocktails, omelettes, fillings for avocado, and sauces for fish are popular everywhere, and pub lunches often include this shellfish delicacy for one-third of what one might pay in other counties. As for the large (Dublin Bay) prawns Cornish trawlers are resuming their traditional fishing off the Scilly Isles to meet the increasing pub demand.

Shrimp Salad

Even a few shrimps are sufficient. Throw some peeled shrimps into a glass dish, folding in slices of hard-boiled eggs and pieces of lettuce heart with a light mayonnaise or a vinaigrette dressing.

Shrimp Pilaf

For Today

A pilaf or pilau is a moist mixture of rice with fish, game or poultry, and in particular a shrimp pilaf is an easy dish for today, hot or cold. Moisten cooked rice with a little fish stock (I mash in some flakes of tinned tuna). Add a few cooked shrimps, folding them into the rice not to break them. Mould individually by packing into small cups or saucers, or into a large mould by packing into a pudding basin. Turn the mould upside down on to a small plate or serving dish as required. Garnish with parsley, lemon segments, or cucumber according to your own taste.

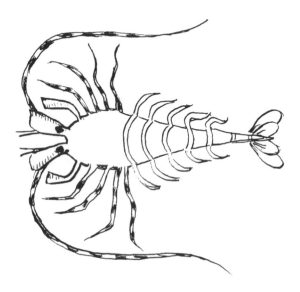

This tiny edible shrimp (enlarged here) was caught in the same net as the prawn on the facing page in one of the Roseland estuaries. The shrimp and prawn were drawn from life by M Daly, Portscatho.

Octopus and Squid

The octopus has eight arms and squid two extra arms or tentacles. Both, dried and fresh, are used in various dishes in Italy and Greece and the flavour resembles lobster. A simple way for cooking squid is to cut the body into thin slices 5 cm or 7 cm (2″ — 3″) thick, pass through flour, egg and crumbs and fry in deep oil or other fat. Beat the tentacles with a mallet and slice and cook them with vegetables. The resultant liquid is reduced and thickened and served with the fried pieces of squid. Not one of my favourites!

What is Scampi?

True scampi consists of the tails of large prawns, creatures in appearance between lobsters and prawns. Whereas in the past fishermen threw them overboard, now — especially the Scottish ports — make a thriving business from these tails, which supplement the imports from Italy. The few caught in Cornish waters are insufficient to warrant 'wholesale' interest for the ever-increasing scampi market.

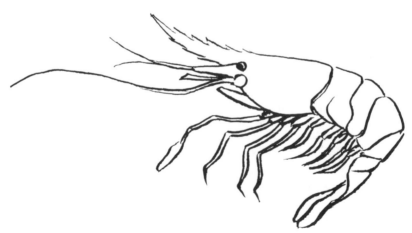

This small prawn, often mistaken for a shrimp, inhabits the estuaries of Cornwall. It is the diminutive cousin of the large sea prawns found off the Isles of Scilly, and is seldom more than two inches long.

IN SEARCH OF A BUSSA

And Many Answers to Many Questions

In a previous chapter you may have been puzzled, as I was, about the various earthenware utensils that seem to have occupied a high status in our kitchens for every purpose, from pickling eggs to the clouting of cream. In other counties metal pots and ovens seem to have taken over earlier while here until well into this century people were well satisfied with their earthenware. To justify our Cornish appreciation of the right way to preserve and cook, using earthenware, is the modern 'slow cooking' pottery casserole of today, lavishly promoted and bought by those sufficiently well off to afford it. Earthenware has a magical quality. Ice, butter, anything to be kept cold, remains that way for many hours and conversely it stands the heat and will retain the heat.

I refer you here to a previous chapter where Shirley Green describes her grandmother taking bussas of marinated mackerel down to the local baker in our village to cook slowly in the embers of his cloam oven at night.

Naturally, to seek a bussa I went to the Cornwall County Museum, at Truro but although they have a world-famous collection of mineral specimens, and Bronze Age burial urns found near Perranporth, not a bussa of any description was to be seen.

Fortunately I found Mr HL Douch's article on *Cornish Earthenware Potters* (Journal of the Royal Institution of Cornwall. Vol VI part 1), which referred to the Lakes of Truro, the only lineal descendants of all the Cornish earthenware potters. When I found the Old Kiln Museum on Chapel Hill I was fascinated and not surprised to hear that when our Prime Minister, Mrs Margaret Thatcher had visited there a few days before she had stayed for two hours.

Mrs Iris Rowse who showed me round the Lake Collection had the answer to so many of my questions. For example, how could Shirley's grandmother have carried one of those big bussas to the local bakery for the gentle night cooking of her marinated mackerel, in the embers of the cloam oven? Mrs Rowse surprisingly replied by heaving the three-foot urn on to her slender shoulder with 'I can carry it — and remember women were stronger in those days!'

Bussa is actually an old Cornish word. In some parts of Cornwall a bussa was known as a stug or stean. They were essentially of the same urn shape but in various sizes.

At the Old Kiln Museum you can see the cloam ovens and the water pitcher called a parrick, presumably designed by Dominican Friary monks at Truro about 1275. All the earthenware utensils our grandmothers used are there, including something I was curious about, that small egg-shaped lamp, the 'chill' or chylla, fuelled by pilchard oil and used in many cottages up to the turn of the century. There, too, are the large pans for the making of clouted cream that I dimly remember as a child in my uncle's farmhouse. There are tongue presses, the barlugg cooking pot that hung over the fire and the crocks — all fashioned from the clay seam found in Truro on the site where the original kiln and museum now stand.

Top left: Bussa made of earthenware in all sizes. Centre: Traditional cloam oven, usually built into an angle of the open fireplace. To the left and right of the oven are the cream pans and parrick or water pitcher. Bottom left is the large salting pan, big enough for parts of the pig. Next to this is the chylla that used pilchard oil for lighting cottage homes. The ubiquitous crock, for cooking in, is at the right.

MEAT, POULTRY AND GAME

Here in our own Peninsula the first farmers owned pigs, oxen, geese and bees. These supplied not only food but lubricants (the bee in the form of wax); reminding me of the important part played by the Cape's hairy fat-tailed sheep in southern Africa whose tail stored fat usually from 15—20 pounds, but in the case of 30 pound tails needing a special crutch made to support it! There it was mutton fat. Here traditional cookery was based on lard. The pig was the backyard all-purpose beast of the landless majority, through the centuries, from the small medieval pig to the big porkers of later times.

Grovey Cake

In origin this might be said to be the Cornish equivalent of Yorkshire pudding, although quite different. After pig-killing, when the fat had been rendered down to lard, the dried groves or scratchings remaining were made into a heavy cake with barley flour and salt to taste. This was cut into pieces and eaten hot. These scratchings were also put over pastry before topping it with meat, apples or both in the sweetmeat tradition of the times.

Sucking pigs were called 'veers' but after 6 or 8 weeks of age were referred to as 'slips'. The pig in a poke (bag) was carried on the shoulder to sell at market. Hamilton Jenkin in his *Cornish Homes and Customs* tells of the market preference for Sancreed pig, leading to the expression 'genuine Sancreed'. Indeed the inhabitants of the little parish of Sancreed were honoured with the name of 'Sancreed Pigs' because their pigs were in such high demand! The reason was that these porkers were dairy fed, while pigs from coastal areas were often fattened on train (pilchard oil) and fish offal.

Now, to a far less extent, our poultry and pigs enjoy a proportion of fish (meal) in their diet which I cannot taste, yet the fussy French declare is 'to fishy for them'. Perhaps our exporters have comments here?

50

Pig Puddings

Hogs pudding, not to be confused with black puddings, made from pigs blood, took the place of our sausages today. Pig skins were soaked in salt and water while pork was put through the mincer with bread, thyme and seasoning, including nutmeg. The dry skins were stuffed tightly then tied up each end and boiled until cooked. They were eaten cold or fried in slices as needed. It was customary to send half of the pig carcass to market and then cure the other half for hams.

The following recipe written delightfully in the descriptive way of the times is but another we acknowledge with gratitude to that 1929 WI Recipe Book:

To Pickle Pork

Hams and Bacon

First go-off be sure you get a healthy pig. Don't buy one from a farmer who expects his sows to keep themselves on whatever they can pick up around the fields and hedges. So, having got your healthy pig, you feed it from the dairy all you can, and keep it in a good condition all the time. This makes a great deal of difference later in the quality of your pork.

Now we will suppose all the unpleasant part of the work is done — you have had liver for supper and liver for breakfast; it was very nice, but you don't want any more. You are ready to tackle the cutting-up and salting away.

You no doubt have assistance for the heavy part of cutting and weighing the separate quarters, but let the salting be your own particular care. Cut up your salt, 14 lbs for a pig weighing 12 or 14 score is a good allowance.— mix in 5 or 6 lbs of moist sugar and two penn'orth of saltpetre. Have a cool or half a barrel clean and dry; sprinkle a layer of salt on the bottom and lay the well-rubbed hams in first, following up with the shoulders and larger pieces of pork and bacon; well sprinkle the salt mixture in all cracks and crevices. Smaller pieces leave till last and after a week these can be taken out and hung up to dry. The hams should be turned, and the brine — which will make itself — occasionally poured over the dry parts. In four weeks take up and allow to drain, then hang in bags near the stove or in any dry place. (St Kea WI)

51

To Boil Ham or Bacon

Soak the smoked ham or bacon in cold water for 4—5 hours and change the water from time to time, depending on the saltiness of the ham. Some hams need hardly any soaking at all. Cover with cold water and bring to the boil and simmer gently with the saucepan lid on until meat is tender right through. (Thirty minutes for 450 g (1 lb) and 30 minutes over.) If the bacon or ham is a thin flat piece cook 25 minutes for 450 g (1 lb) with 25 minutes over. For serving cold, leave it in water until cool when the rind can be removed and you can add the raspings of bread or glaze used to coat the outside.

Boiled Pork with Cider

And Pease Pudding

For this traditional meal the joint of pork was brought to the boil in a big pan full of water, and simmered for some time until half cooked, with peppercorns and seasoning. Then vegetables were added, such as turnips, onions, carrots, a cabbage quartered, celery tops and any vegetable, it is said, except potatoes. Two handfuls of dried peas with a sprig of mint were put into a bag big enough to allow them to swell in cooking. The bag was tied with string and suspended inside the pan with the pork, a spoon of treacle and a cup or two of cider were added and the whole simmered on top of the stove for some hours.

For serving, the pork was strained and dished up with the vegetables. The peas, which should have swollen into a large ball shape, were unrolled and served with the pork. The broth was poured over the pork and the pudding served as an accompaniment.

To Roast Pork

Wipe meat with a damp cloth and bone it if required. Stuff the gap with sage and onion stuffing. Skewer or tie strongly into shape. Place in a roasting pan, brushed with oil, to sear in a hot oven for 15 minutes. Then reduce heat to moderate, 200°C (400°F). Baste every 20 minutes if an uncovered pan is used. With a self-basting covered roasting pan uncover the last 20 minutes to crispen. For crisper brown crackling brush joint with oil and brandy and place under grill while gravy is being made. Serve with thick gravy and apple sauce.

To score pork for crackling — if the butcher has not scored the skin — use a sharp pointed knife and with the point slit the skin in lines ½″ between each, right across the surface of the meat.

Suckling or Sucking Pig

In former times tiny pigs of 3 weeks old were roasted side by side after being fattened with milk and barley meal. Today a chef considers the veer should not be more than 6 weeks old. Wash and dry, sprinkle inside with brandy, season inside and out. Stuff with (a) chicken livers, mushrooms, onions, parsley, dill, marjoram, tarragon butter, seasoned with pepper and salt and raw eggs for binding. (b) Breadcrumbs, grated lemon rind, suet, sage, seasoning and egg to bind. When stuffed sew up with strong thread. Truss with forelegs skewered back, and hindlegs forward. Brush with oil and roast in a deep pan in a moderately hot oven. Serve with an apple in the mouth, a purée of potatoes, baked apples filled with raisins, etc. If a plump appearance is important such as buffet display, stuff part of the body with a loaf of white bread, but do not serve this, of course.

Baked Ham

With Cider

After soaking the ham, wipe dry. Make a stiff paste of flour and water, completely coating the ham in this to hold in the juices. Put in a hot oven until the huff hardens, then reduce heat for a moderate oven for 4 or 5 hours. Twice during this period make a hole in the top of the crust and pour in a cup of hot cider. When cooked remove the crust, skin ham, brush with egg and breadcrumbs, then brown the coating in the oven. Serve hot or cold.

The traditional accompaniment for hot ham and pork was peas pudding but spiced crab apples, mustard and gooseberry purée were popular.

Ham out of a Tin

With Black Cherry Glaze

1 kg (2·205 lb) tin of ham, a large can of black cherries, 2½ teaspoons cornflour, 2 tablespoons of port.

Remove any gelatine from outside of ham. Drain cherries, put syrup in saucepan. Blend one tablespoon of the syrup with cornflour, add to saucepan with port. Stir over heat until sauce boils and thickens. Arrange cherries on top of ham, pour glaze over.

Sauce for Spare Ribs

Roasted spare ribs may be served garnished with grilled bacon rolls and a sauce made by simmering 1 can condensed tomato soup, 2 teaspoons of Worcestershire sauce, 1 clove of crushed garlic, a teaspoon of mixed dried herbs and a dash of vinegar.

Brawn from Pork

Half a pig's head (brains removed), seasoned well with herbs in a bag, formed the basis of the farmwife's brawns, requiring no addition to jellify the result. In the following recipe the old rules are waived, avoiding conveniently coming face to half-face with the pig.

Brawn

Today's Version

Instead of giving one of the old recipes here is Lesley's own modern version using shin of beef and trotters, those from sheep, not pigs!

680 g (1½ lb) shin of beef, 4 sheep's trotters, 1 onion (cut up small), 2 teaspoons dried herbs, 1 bunch parsley, pinch of sugar, salt, MSG and pepper.

Wash the trotters and put them on to boil with water. When they are about half done add the beef and the cut-up onion. Add a little more water if necessary. Cook until meat comes away from the bones. Discard the bones and cut all meat up into small pieces. Then add sugar, salt, pepper and MSG to taste. Have ready 2 tablespoon of gelatine melted in ½ cup of cold water over hot water. Add herbs and parsley. Mix altogether. If liked decorate the mould with hard-boiled egg slices. Leave in the refrigerator and turn out when required.

Back to Pot-Roasting

Why waste fuel by roasting a small joint in the oven? You can get good results by pot-roasting, on the top of the stove, as brown and succulent as desired. To pot-roast choose a heavy saucepan, heat about 1½″ of fat in the bottom until a slight blue smoke rises (but be sure the fat doesn't burn). Tie meat or poultry into a neat shape and lower into the hot fat, turning until golden brown all over. Reduce heat from low to moderate (depending on quantity), and allow the joint to cook, basting from time to time. When joint is tender, make the gravy by pouring off the fat in the usual way and thickening the sediment in the pot.

Our old-time sheep have been described 'having grey faces and legs, short thick necks, narrow backs, flattish sides and a fleece of coarse wool (Cornish hair)'. Living upon the downs summer and winter their mutton was said to be good. More aristocratic than these so-called mongrel breeds was the sheep found on the north coast whose flesh and fleece were good. 'This superiority was ascribed to their liking for the small snails which appear on the sandy surface of the towans morning and evening.' (*Cornish Homes and Customs* David and Charles Ltd.)

Goat & Kid

Goats meat and milk were the privilege of the rich, the poor making money by fattening the goats and selling them at Christmas markets. Although roast kid is referred to as a luxury, goats meat is almost ignored in our old cook books, albeit goats hair was used in the process of cider making. As for mutton it is played down by old cook books that reserve their enthusiasm for various squab pies with mutton chops as a substitute for young pigeons (squabs).

Lamb

A lamb was a special treat in the spring and boiled mutton flavoured with rosemary and parsley was served with caper sauce, often made with nasturtium seeds taking the place of imported capers. (See Index).

Today New Zealand lamb has undercut our Cornish lamb, and as for mutton, one hardly hears the word nowadays. Just as 'chicken' has supplanted 'hen' in recipes, so 'lamb' has 'mutton'. Our local lamb is the best.

Stuffed Shoulder

Stuffing extends the lamb into 'family' class. Ask the butcher to de-bone the joint, and then stuff with a forcemeat mixture that includes mint, breadcrumbs, chopped onions, grated rind of lemon and rosemary bound with an egg. Tie neatly and roast or wrap in foil, shiny side in, and cook slowly at 120°C (250°F) for 3—4 hours for a 1.85 kg (4 lb) joint, unwrapping the foil for the last 30 minutes to crispen the meat.

Cunning Kebabs

For your Barbecue

Kebabs appeal to all ages. From those steak house addicts who slide the succulent cubes of fillet alternated with mushrooms on to their plates — to the young fry who tear off the cubed scraps with their teeth from imaginary swords. The skewers are easily obtainable and the meat goes twice as far this kebab way. It is important to pack the skewers so that the contents don't disintegrate and there's some art, too, in selecting the skewered foods in happy combinations. Remember the skewers get hot and a kitchen mitt is essential in this form of cookery. Remember, too, that the cubes of meat and meat balls shrink in the cooking, therefore they should be large enough to thread on the skewers without breaking. Mutton cubes may be alternated with cubes of apple, cooked sweet potato, green pepper and pineapple. Pickles, especially rounds of the dill type go with most meats and any ham, rolled or cubed, as well.

The meats may be marinated or not before being partly cooked under a grill, then threaded on to the skewers with the selected oddments; all of which are brushed with oil or the marinade (which has oil in it) and browned on the skewers. Select foods that keep their shape and colour. I've seen a picnic meal: hors d'ouvre, fish roast, pud and fruit all on one skewer!

Beef . . . . Traditional

When You Can Afford It

The well-cared-for ox, answering to his own name and sometimes shod by the blacksmith, ultimately provided good meat for the farmer, and no-one seemed to grumble at the age of the beast. Veal was sold to the gentry and precious little steak came the labourer's way. There were 'feasten' occasions of course when labourers made up for lean months, as indicated by the itemised Midsummer dinner given at a beershop for china clay workers in the parish of Roche. The party consisted of 16 men, 9 boys and 5 females who consumed: 90 lb beef and pork, 3/6 worth of old potatoes, 7/6 worth of household bread, 1/6 worth of cabbage and 150 quarts of beer, together with 14 oz of tobacco. We are left wondering how they got through 3 lb of meat each.

Today our times are now out of joint we might say, roasting joints having outpriced themselves. Those saucer-sized joints that families sit round at table today cannot be compared with the barons of beef on the giant platter of the past. But let's cheer up, there is still . . . .

Cornish Under Roast

Which way you make this typical Cornish casserole depends on the type of meat you have (tender or tough). The former is bedded down in the oven dish raw, while the latter is simmered until tender before being baked. Basically, the meat is cut into strips and rolled in seasoned flour, then topped with layers of thickly cut potatoes, brushed with bacon fat or oil. A little water or stock is usually added and some recipes suggest using a cut-up ox kidney, onion and mushrooms, all according to taste. The under roast is baked in a moderate oven until the potatoes are brown. Naturally, when raw meat is used the cooking time is longer.

Crispy Cornish Sausages

Wash and prick each sausage. Soak in a little milk for 5 minutes or more. Dip into self-raising flour. Fry in a little oil, turning until golden brown and cooked through. Or grill, basting with oil until brown. Serve on potato mash with grilled tomatoes or a purée of apples or gooseberries. The milk? Use as a gravy base or for Kitty.

Steak remains the most popular cut of beef, especially when it is rump or fillet grilled to perfection; but stewing steak and cheaper cuts have returned to favour.

Steak and Beer

2 lb stewing steak, ½ lb bacon, 1 large onion, 2 tablespoons apple or red currant jelly, 1 pint beer, a pinch of sugar.

Fry the chopped onion until soft. Add the cut-up bacon, cook, and remove to the side of the pan while browning the meat, which has been coated with seasoned flour (use MSG **not** salt — see Index). Place the meat, bacon and onion in a casserole, add the jelly to the beer and pour over the meat mixture. Put on the lid and cook in a slow oven at 120°C (250°F) until tender. Serve topped with croutons of fried bread, with prepared boiled rice, peas and a green salad. If you use the frozen variety of peas, prepare them in the following way: Just pop the frozen peas with their own icicles into a saucepan without any water, add a little salt, a pinch of sugar, pat of butter and a sprig of mint. Cook until just soft.

Shin and Oxtail Casserole

1 oxtail, 450 g (1 lb) shin, 2 onions, gravy browning, sliced potatoes, sliced carrots, oil for frying, stock, salt and pepper.

Fry onions lightly in oil and place in casserole with the shin and oxtail; add stock and seasoning and place in a low oven and leave as long as possible. If left all night as low as the oven will go, it can be taken out in the morning and put in the refrigerator. When required, remove all fat and then add vegetables and cook in oven until they are done. The shin absorbs all the flavour of the oxtail and will give you far more meat to eat.

Good Old-fashioned Stew

Gone Modern

680 g (1½ lb) shin and neck of beef, 225 g (½ lb) bacon, 2 apples, peeled and chopped, 2 onions, chopped, 4 tomatoes, peeled and sliced, 2 green or red peppers, sliced (optional), 450 ml (¾ pint) water, 2 beef cubes, a tablespoon of Worcester sauce, 2 bay leaves and thyme to taste, 6 carrots.

Fry bacon, chop and put in a saucepan. Using the bacon fat, fry the apples and onions together and remove to saucepan. Add a little oil to the frypan and fry the sliced peppers and tomatoes. Cube the meat, flour and brown it quickly in the pan with the greasing of the fat that remains, and put it in the saucepan with all the other ingredients adding 450 ml (¾ pint) of water with the beef cubes, bay leaves and thyme. Bring to boil and simmer for as long as possible, at least for 3 hours. Add the carrots about half an hour before the dish is ready.

Boiled Silverside

Spicy Old Recipe

1·35 kg—1·8 kg (3—4 lb) salted silverside, 2 teaspoons allspice, 2 teaspoons dry mustard, a tablespoon brown sugar, water to barely cover, 1 clove-stuck onion.

Wash the meat then rub with spice, mustard and brown sugar. Place in a saucepan with vinegar and onion, tipping in the balance of any loose spice, mustard and sugar. Bring to the boil slowly and simmer 30 minutes to each 450 g (1 lb) and 30 minutes over. Serve hot with carrots, onions and wedges of cabbage added 25 minutes before meat is cooked. If required cold leave the meat to cool in the cooking water. This is ideal for sandwiches.

Mincing Matters

Mince, made with pestle and mortar, was popular for all kinds of dishes in medieval times because of general lack of teeth. Even kings with teeth (supplied by their serfs), partook of gruesomely dyed highly spiced dishes composed of a mixture of meats and fruit but surviving in our **good** Christmas mincemeat. Alas, butcher's mince today is not as good as it should be and almost always far too fat. (But hats off to **Marks and Spencer** for their lean minced beef!) Here, reprinted from my book *Let's Win the Cooking Game*, subtitled 'living like a millionaire for a few pence a portion' is my own basic mince mixture, used for hamburgers, meat loaves, meat balls and, with milk added, for cottage pies.

Basic Mince Mixture

450 g (1 lb) topside mince with no fat, one sliced onion, 1 or 2 rashers of streaky bacon, 2 teaspoons salt, one teaspoon pepper, ⅛ teaspoon MSG, ½ teaspoon freshly grated nutmeg, a dash of Worcestershire sauce, ½ teaspoon of powdered mustard, milk to mix (**no eggs**).

Fry the finely chopped onion with the chopped de-rinded bacon rashers in a very little butter and oil until both are half cooked. Add this with the fat from the pan to the minced meat in a bowl, mixing in well all the other ingredients. Add milk as needed to make into a thick (barely dropping) consistency. Do not use eggs, as they toughen raw meats. Eggs, however, are needed to bind **already cooked** meat mince and where much vegetable and cereal has been used with the meat to extend it.

Making ends 'meat'

BIRDS FOR THE TABLE

How different is the plump chicken we roast in half an hour today to the scrawny old hen that sizzled in the crock or on the spit for hours on the open hearths of yesteryear! And in case someone jumps in to correct me about the cooking time of chicken (½—¾ hour according to size) I hasten to add I use my self-basting roasting pan with lid and the end result is as brown and crisp as the open pan method that needs tiresome basting. The lid is removed for the last ten minutes, of course, for crispening.

One Chicken Roasted

Many Meals

Here is an economical way of using one or more birds. Immediately after buying remove giblets, wash out interior and throw coarse salt into cavity until required for roasting. To roast, wipe over with vinegar or lemon juice and stuff with seasoned poultry stuffing or merely place halved small onions, peppers, rice or potatoes, and/or tomatoes — with or without a pinch of herbs — in cavity. (Some purists ban onion in chicken.) Dredge with seasoned flour and place bird in a covered baking tin or self-basting roasting pan in a very hot oven for 15 minutes, then a moderate oven for about 30 minutes for a small chicken; then remove lid to crispen outside.

For Cocktail Snacks: place around the bird the chicken liver sliced, seasoned and wrapped in streaky bacon tied with thread. These dainty rolls can be sliced when cold and used to top mayonnaised water biscuits or croutons, and then glazed. Protect them from crisping with foil and remove at half time. Glazed did I say? Most cocktail snacks become more appetising when brushed with home-made aspic. They keep better too.

Seasoned pumpkin slices, potatoes, turnips and onions can be roasted round the chicken at the same time. In a covered roasting tin all can be cooked in less than ¾ hour. To increase the flavour of chicken the skin can be lifted before cooking and layered with seasoning such as garlic, salt, pepper and MSG (see Index), then replaced; or bacon rashers may be placed on top before or at the crispening stage. Moist stuffing helps to tenderize chicken.

An entire repertoire of recipes, hot and cold, relate to left-overs of chicken (or other poultry) cooked as above, but suffice it to say I simply dare not omit the essential . . . .

Stock from Chicken Carcass

Court Bouillon

This is the secret of good cooking. Just as fish bones and scraps can be boiled for a few minutes to give valuable fumet for fish sauces so can the chicken carcass, which needs not more than ¾ hour. Just throw the carcass and all chicken scraps, bits of stuffing and gravy into a saucepan adding a few herbs if stuffing is not included. Strain and leave in the fridge overnight, then skim off fat — which is ideal for French bread and sautéed potatoes for the family. Store the resultant jelly until required for adding to minced dishes or pies, gravies and soups, and so on. This also forms the basis of a court bouillon with vegetables, but avoid using potatoes.

Roast Duck Today

Easy way is to fill with sage and onion stuffings and roast on a bed of bacon rashers, topped with streaky bacon and foiled; or in a self-basting roaster with lid, removing cover the last ten minutes to brown and crispen. Most people prefer duck well done, but in France specially fed succulent ducks are served slightly pink. For roast duck, when the breast is served rare in French style, the thighs will be underdone. They are usually detached, cooked further under the grill and then passed as a second helping.

Duckling is monotonously served with orange on menus yet a truly Cornish way is to serve it with glazed turnips. Chefs cut the turnips to baby size and scatter a little brown sugar over when they bake. Tiny onions and a wine sauce provide a welcome change. Chefs ring another change with duck by an accompaniment of Morello cherries (pitted) and wine added to the juices of the pan. If you must have Duck à l'orange you can stuff the duck with a whole unpeeled orange and a sauce made with lemon juice added to strained orange marmalade. If orange is served as an accompaniment cut it into pith-free segments.

Goose and Turkey

The Christmas bird seems to have originated in the St Michaelmas feast of September 29th to celebrate the harvest. It was a goose, and in line with its important by-products — including valuable grease as a basis for ointments and cosmetics — goes way back to the earliest times.

Because the Michaelmas goose was fattened on stubble and gleanings left by the reapers and young rabbit were at their best at the same time and for the same reason, it is not surprising to find recipes for goose and rabbit cooked together, the fat of the former lubricating the dry flesh of the latter.

In time goose became **the** bird for Christmas with different stuffings at each end. For example, the crop might be stuffed with sausage meat and potatoes and the body of the bird filled with a delectable stuffing of liver, breadcrumbs, apples, onions, chopped sage and nutmeg. Secured to the spit or trussed and baked (we use foil or a self-basting roasting pan today) it was uncovered at intervals and basted with rough cider. It was served with apple or gooseberry purée, made from the housewife's dried apples or preserve. A green (young) goose was usually left unstuffed but apples could be put inside.

If your goose is too large for the oven do as I do with too big a turkey, as suggested in Turkey Tips further on.

Turkey is the latest bird on the Christmas scene, given impetus to popularity no doubt by its part in the commemoration of the Pilgrim Fathers' celebration of the Plymouth Colony's first harvest in 1621 by roasting four wild turkeys. But it was not until 1941, by resolution of Congress that Thanksgiving Day was officially recognised to be kept on the first Thursday in November. Here sales indicate Turkey a truly festive bird. It may be stuffed as for goose. Favourite crop stuffings include chestnuts or mushrooms.

Turkey Tips for Today

Be sure the frozen turkey you buy at the supermarket is allowed to thaw sufficiently before it is cooked; this may take 2 or 3 days. If the bird is too large for your oven don't worry. Cut off the legs, with the thigh if necessary, then stuff and roast your turkey as usual while the legs simmer on top of the stove, or in a casserole below. Assemble the turkey on a serving dish, using skewers to hold the bird in proper shape. Mask the joins and leg parts with glaze or gravy or grilled bacon, while the body part is left crisp and golden brown as it should be. As a matter of fact the limbs, being more tender, the bird goes further this way.

LIVING HIGH . . . . GAME

While the farmer could shoot or snare on his own lands the average labourer was precluded by the poaching laws from tasting much wild life. But Christmas was usually the big exception, when workers participated with farmers or gentry in eating some of the game they had helped their masters bring down that season. When you visit an historic home, in imagination you see the great open fireplace in the hall stacked with logs of ash, elm and bog turf and in front of this raging fire there are the spits, sometimes small spits, for the various little items such as fish, hare and birds, but more often a giant spit supported at each end by two sturdy dog irons. These giant spits could carry joints of venison, piglets and large meats, below which the small game cooked in the dripping pans; hare, pheasant, snipe, woodcock and such.

Visiting historic homes, I seek out the kitchen and hall to discover just what kind of spit was used. So many ingenious ways of locomotion were employed, from the old hand-turned ones to the ventilation variety and the one that always makes me a little sad, the treadmill for a 'spits dog'. (My dachshund I chose to call by her true breed, an English spits dog.)

But back to game, beginning with that all-important venison, always well hung and varying from the tender red deer to the large red stags which required marinating, larding and wrapping in foil to ensure their succulence:

Roast Venison

For the Marinade:

1 teaspoon cloves, 1 teaspoon allspice, 2 tablespoons brown sugar, 2 tablespoons salt, 1 teaspoon pimento, 1 bottle port wine.

For larding: a few cloves of garlic, 250 g (½ lb) fat bacon.

Mix the sugar, salt and spices. Take 1 teaspoon of this mixture and mix well into ½ cup of the port. To lard the venison, use a sharp long-bladed knife to pierce several holes in the meat, along the grain of the meat. Open up each hole with the finger and pour a teaspoon of the wine and spice mixture into it. (Stir the wine to keep the spices well mixed.) Now push a small piece of garlic into each hole, then a strip of fat bacon. Rub the rest of the spice mixture into the meat. Pour some of the wine into a suitable basin and place the venison in this to marinate for 48 hours, or longer, basting frequently with the liquid. Leave in the refrigerator. When required, simmer venison in the rest of the wine until nearly tender, then roast it in the oven, spread with butter until brown. Serve with quince or red currant jelly.

Accompanying vegetables included turnips (translated by 'furr-iners' as swedes) and Roscoff broccoli and winter cauliflower. A master chef tells me his good gravy secret with venison is to add a cube or two of the best bitter chocolate.

Jugged Hare

One hare, cut up, seasoned flour, 450 g (1 lb) onions, 5 cloves, peel of one lemon, 2 glasses port wine (or strong cider), 1 tablespoon mushroom ketchup, butter, a little flour.

Dredge the hare pieces with seasoned flour and a little cayenne. Peel the onions and slice all but one and stick this one with the cloves. Put the hare into a stone jar or deep casserole, add all the onions and the lemon peel. Cover with water or, better still, a good stock. (In less expensive times the stock was made from a pound of steak.) Cover the jar closely to keep the steam from escaping. Set the jar in a deep stewpan of cold water and let it simmer for 4 hours, on top of the stove or in the oven. When the hare is really tender and 'almost leaving the bones', add the wine or cider, the ketchup and a knob of butter in which a dessertspoon of flour has been worked. Cook until the gravy has thickened. Serve with redcurrant jelly and forcemeat balls.

Rabbit may be cooked, following chicken recipes.

Game Birds

Most game birds are improved by larding, but if you are not skilled with a larding needle just wrap a good thick rasher of very fat bacon round each bird. The bacon must be removed for the last ten minutes of roasting time. Reluctantly I must omit the recipes for various game birds but the following are traditionally imperative:

Braised Pigeons

Squab is an old word for pigeon, going back to the time when pigeon-cotes were a feature of every sizeable garden. The breeding of pigeons declined when farmers objected to them consuming their crops, but squab pie lived on and could be based on any young bird, or no bird at all as, for example, the squab pie made from mutton in our **Pies** chapter. For braised pigeons:

> 2 pigeons, 100 g (4 oz) bacon rashers, 1 carrot, salt, pepper, 1 onion, a stalk of celery, 150 g (6 oz) butter, a clove of garlic, bayleaf, sprig of thyme, ½ glass of white wine or cider, ½ glass chicken stock (or cube).

Chop all but two rashers of bacon, and the vegetables, into thin strips, and colour in the butter in a pan, sprinkling on the seasoning, thyme and chopped garlic; lay the bayleaf on top. Wrap the birds in the two remaining rashers, and lay them in the pan, add the wine and the bouillon. Simmer gently for 30 minutes.

Monkey with Turnspit. Sketched from an original coloured manuscript (Flemish, circ. AD 1300) by Brenda Lighton, with permission of the Trustees of the British Museum.

OFFAL

Les Abats or Variety Meats

The American term 'variety meats' is my choice, but the French do not flinch at *abats* and here we use the word offal when forced to do so. It includes sweetbreads, brains, hearts, tripe and importantly liver — valuable through the ages in the treatment for anaemia.

The customary use of fresh offal through necessity when a beast was slaughtered to be salted must have contributed valuable nourishment to a family's diet at least once or twice a year.

Sweetbreads

And a Cornishism Discovered

Naturally, we think of starting off with sweetbreads, as the sweetest offal of all; but, strictly speaking, these are not classed as offal, being the thymus gland of a lamb or calf and consisting of two parts, connected by membrane or tubing. The round compact part is called the 'heart sweetbread' as its position is nearer the heart; the other part is called the 'throat sweetbread'.

When sweetbreads are separated at market, avoid buying two throat sweetbreads as the heart sweetbread is more desirable. Those sold by the butcher were usually veal sweetbreads. This gland is pre-natally developed for, as soon as the calf is taken from liquid food, it begins to disappear. Strangely, only in oxen does a usable part of the heart 'bread' persist into adult life. As sweetbreads spoil very quickly, buy them just before they are to be cooked.

When I inquired about the scarcity of sweetbreads today, a Truro butcher seemed embarrassed and sought refuge behind his block, leaving his wife to answer my questions. She said with a smile, 'It is easier for me to explain, "being a woman".' 'Why?' I asked, perplexed. 'Well you see half our sweetbreads are lambs' testicles,' she said.

Further inquiry confirmed this to be common in Cornwall and probably here sweetbreads may indicate other delicate morsels? Certainly the pancreas is sometimes sold as part of a pair of sweetbreads. Please don't ask me why the butcher was embarrassed. I know not.

To Cook Sweetbreads

Remove from the paper as soon as possible, plunge them into cold water and allow them to remain in the water for one hour. Drain, put into warm salted water, adding 2 tablespoons of lemon juice or vinegar. Cook them for 20 minutes, then drain and plunge into cold water to keep them white and firm. Trim inedible parts. Dredge with seasoned flour, dip them in oil and broil under the griller, basting with a little of the stock in which they were cooked, until they are brown. Serve with gooseberry purée on rice, or potatoes mashed with turnips — truly Cornish.

Marinated Brains and Sweetbreads

675 g (1½ lb) brains and sweetbreads, 1 cup white vinegar, salt and pepper, 2 bay leaves, 3 cloves garlic, 1 small onion sliced.

Soak brains and sweetbreads in salted water for an hour. Remove and put into boiling water and cook until tender (about 5 minutes). Drain and remove any membrane and cut in slices. Pour vinegar in a pan and add all other ingredients. Bring to boil, reduce heat and add brains and sweetbreads. Simmer 5 minutes longer. Keep overnight before serving cold.

Tripe

If not prepared by the butcher this requires a lot of cleaning, scrubbing and trimming. For the characteristic delicate flavour, bring to the boil in water to which has been added a few drops of lemon juice; throw away the water, adding fresh cold water and repeat the process as many as three times, until tripe is tender.

Tripe and Onions

Add squares of neatly cut-up cooked tripe to plenty of tiny onions previously cooked in stock (or a chicken cube added to water). Season well with salt and pepper and heat all up. Remove from stove and add ¾ cup cream and 3 egg yolks previously beaten together. Combine with the tripe and onion mixture and keep hot over hot water (eg the top of a double saucepan) until required.

Heart

Calf, Ox, Sheep

Wash well in cold water, cut away membrane and tough flaps, squeeze out any blood. Leave to soak in fresh water for 1 hour. Discard this water, dry heart before cooking. Roast slowly or braise. Bake a calf's heart for from 1—1½ hours, a young ox heart for about 2½—3 hours, a sheep's heart for about 2 hours.

Pigs Fry

Immediately the pig was killed the blood was drained off for the popular black pudding (to be dried) and what became known as pig's fry, consisting of the heart, liver, lights and sweetbread. These were simmered in salted water for half an hour then cut up neatly and fried in hot fat. Another meal was made of the fry by baking it in a dish layered with potatoes. All was well seasoned with herbs added.

Fried Brains and Beef Marrow

Cut the sheep brains into pieces and add the marrow dug out of a beef bone. Roll in seasoned flour, then in beaten egg and breadcrumbs. Fry in a mixture of butter and oil. Some prefer to coat the pieces with a batter made with water, flour, cheese and beaten egg, seasoned to taste.

Crumbed Sheep Brains

Allowing a set of brains per person, skin under running water and simmer for 5 minutes. This blanching of the brains may be done the day before. Remove from heat, dry, dredge in flour, dip in milk or milk and beaten egg. Roll in breadcrumbs and fry golden brown in a little hot oil. Serve with bacon for breakfast.

Poor Man's Goose

450 g (1 lb) liver, 1 tablespoon flour, 100 g (¼ lb) bacon, ½ teaspoon powdered sage, 2 small par-boiled onions, salt, pepper, 2 par-boiled potatoes, dripping.

Cut liver into thin slices and dip in seasoned flour. Chop onions and slice potatoes thinly. Cut bacon into pieces. Place alternate layers of liver, onions, seasoning, bacon and potato, putting dabs of dripping on the potato layer. Add a little water, about ¼ cup. Cover casserole and bake at 190°C (375°F) for 1½ hours.

Little Liver Cakes

250 g (½ lb) lamb or calves liver, 2 streaky bacon rashers and one small chopped onion, 1 cup cold cooked and mashed potatoes, 1 teaspoon Worcestershire sauce, 1 tablespoon finely chopped parsley, salt and pepper.

Fry lightly the liver with the bacon and onion in a little oil. Then put through the mincer, using a lemon rind to clean mincer — a few grains of which can be mixed with the liver. Add the minced mixture to the cold mashed potatoes.

Hot Beef Tongue

To cook ox tongue that has been salted, wash and soak overnight in cold water. Curl the tongue round a skewer then place in a large saucepan with 2 onions, 2 carrots, a bay leaf and 6 peppercorns. Cover and simmer for about 3½ hours or until the small bones at the base of the tongue come away easily and the skin is ready to peel off. Transfer the tongue to a board, remove the skewer, peel off the skin and discard bones and gristle. Tie or skewer and serve hot with onion and tomato sauce.

Pressed Ox Tongue — Cold

Prepare tongue as above but remove skewer and curl round tightly to fit a casserole or soufflé dish. Dissolve 2 level teaspoons gelatine in 2 tablespoons cold water. Strain ½ cup hot stock in which tongue was cooked and stir this into the gelatine and water until dissolved. Colour with a little browning if required. Pour this liquid over tongue in the dish. Put dish on a large plate, cover with a small plate over tongue and then put a heavy weight on the plate. Leave in fridge to set. To serve, remove plate and weight, hold in hot water for ½ minute and invert on to a serving dish. Slice thinly.

Lamb's Tongue

With Almond Sauce

Wash 4 lambs' tongues and simmer in a court bouillon, (see method for Ox Tongue as above) until tender. Drain but keep the stock and peel off the skin. Make a roux from ¼ cup butter and 2 tablespoons flour, dilute with ½ pint strained stock from the tongue liquid, simmer gently, stirring continually. Add ⅔ cup ground almonds, 3 tablespoons seedless raisins, salt and pepper, 2 tablespoons lemon juice, a pinch of sugar and a sprinkling of MSG. Slice the tongues lengthways, arrange on a serving dish, pour the almond sauce over, serve hot.

To Sour Cream

This May be Bought

To sour cream for recipes demanding it, add lemon or vinegar to fresh cream in the proportion of 2 teaspoons lemon juice or 1 teaspoon vinegar to 1 cup cream. Or add 2 tablespoons buttermilk to 1 cup cream and allow to stand at room temperature until sour cream develops naturally.

THE PASTY AND PIES

So many people outside Cornwall have written so much about the Cornish pasty we are in danger of going down into history as having invented nothing else, rather like the Swiss and their cuckoo clock. Yet it was well worthwhile inventing.

Our foremothers, who started the pasty off and their female descendants who have brought it to what it is today — a keen rival of the hamburger and the sandwich — were smart enough to give birth to a meal in the hand for those ploughing the earth, working under it, or sailing the sea. Whereas sandwiches tend to be either soggy or dry the Cornish pasty is neither. The firm pastry ensures the filling is fresh and moist and if well made it tastes as good cold as hot; although to eat my words, an old villager told me that as a child she was made to 'run quickly' to the fields to be sure Dad got his pasty hot.

The pasty, or ogee, in fact, is a triumph of Cornish make-do.

How did our pasty originate and evolve into the classic snack of today? Among many old books on cooking I own one fondly treasured, entitled *Old Cookery Books and Ancient Cuisine by W Carew Hazlitt* (Elliott Stock 1886). He happens to be an ancestor on my mother's side with our common ancestry of William Hazlitt, the essayist. He actually refers to our pasty. When describing the making of the ancient bag pudding from barley meal, raisins and hog's blood — which it has been said was served by King Arthur himself at the Court of Camelot — Hazlitt suggests the bag pudding was the 'culinary forefather of toad-in-the-hole. hot-pot, Irish stew and of that devil-dreaded Cornish pasty'.

As for Hazlitt's awareness of the Devil's fear of crossing the Tamar, it was indeed devilish difficult to cross it in the old days and even within recent memory (before the Toll bridge), when cars queued to get across the ferry morning and night. And, as suggested before, the Devil would surely not think it worth the effort to come to a county so abundantly blessed with saints.

Pasties appear to have been born about the end of the 18th century and the first often consisted of vegetables within a dark barley corn crust. Fillings, as listed further on for pies, were padded out with barley and even the bones of the animal such as a rabbit carcass to make them acceptably plump. Sometimes the pasty was not baked in the ubiquitous iron pot but wrapped up in a cabbage leaf and steamed over soup or anything set to boil on the fire. An 18th century visitor observed 'the labourers in general bring up their families with only potatoes or turnip or leeks or peppergrass rolled up in a black barley crust'. (*St James Chronicle: Soup on Sundays.*)

The miners' common hoggan was unleavened dough in which were vegetables with an occasional prize of a piece of green (young) pork. The miner, earning in the 1840s about £2.50 a month, insisted on something to stand up to his surroundings as is aptly expressed by Mr Herbert Thomas in his well known song:

'Aw, you don't want fancy denners when you're sweaten bare your bones,
An' feel as ef you could digest a barraful of stones,
'Tes for somethin' braave and solid that you know your sperit groans,
And a hoggan like stull tember you could chow, comrade.'

Fuggan

Cake or Pasty?

This oval-shaped sugarless cake was turned into a pasty on occasions, and the old recipe includes the use of sour milk or buttermilk to bind the ingredients:

Two ounces of lard or suet were rubbed into 2 cups of flour with a pinch of salt and a handful of currants added. After mixing with sour milk or buttermilk the fuggan was rolled about 1″ thick, marked with a knife across and baked for half an hour.

Meaty Fuggan

The currants for this are omitted and the oval shape opened in the middle to stuff with fresh chopped-up pork or beef, well seasoned. Pinched to close it pasty-wise, it was baked in a hot oven for 35 minutes.

Among my collection of pasties are the following; and all to be made with relevant seasoning as required.

Meat and Potato Pasty: Fresh steak cubed, with onion and potato.

Pork Pasty: Fresh pork and potatoes, enhanced by sliced cooking apples, onions and sage.

Rabbit Pasty: Best fleshy part of rabbit cut up similarly to steak.

Chicken Pasty: Cut-up chicken with mushrooms and bacon scraps.

Mutton Pasty: Mutton cut-up with potatoes and much parsley.

Stargazy Pasty: Herring was stuffed with a savoury forcemeat and arranged with the head out of the pasty one side and tail t'other.

Mackerel Pasty: Clean and boil mackerel. Removing skin and bones, put white flesh on pasty. Sprinkle with lemon juice, add some fronds of parsley then season and pinch up in usual way.

Rice Pasty: Use any left-over rice pudding, add a few raisins and fill the short crust pastry.

Blackberry and Apple Pasty: Mix thinly sliced apples with fresh blackberries and sprinkle with brown sugar.

Farmer's Favourite: An extra long pasty filled with seasoned meat one end and sugared apples or jam the other. A partition to separate the two courses of the meal was achieved by making a little roll of pastry between the meat and fruit.

'A pasty a day' was the axiom of workers in the fields and mines, and even at the present time the pasty more than holds its own for picnic fare, plus almost any other good excuse to make it and eat it. When our bus goes to Plymouth and Exeter on occasions, many of my fellow travellers are armed with pasties, the appetising aroma of which declares we are Cornish and on a Cornish bus.

Countrywide Controversies

The traditional Cornish pasty ignores the snobby richness of puff paste. Every pastry maker has her own favourite recipe, born of her own family usually, and one that will stand the test of travel. But there are two schools of thought about three things. Firstly, side crimping or middle crimping? Secondly, should the 'taties' be cubed or sliced? Thirdly, to glaze or not to glaze?

The consensus around here is that crimping should be in the middle of the pasty, to hold the gravy. The potato, when sliced, thinly forming top and bottom layers with the meat in between, helps to make the steam that makes the gravy, which in this layered fashion is distributed more evenly. The glazing, which in the old days was done with saffron-milk and now with egg and milk, certainly does make the pasty look more appetising. As some judges of pasties are at variance themselves over the above points it is wise to seek out a judge's preference before submitting a pasty for 'show'.

With reluctance to throw the cat among more pigeons in this culinary controversy, here are recipes from Cornishwomen who, while using different methods for their pasty making, are still the best of friends! Their products are certainly superior to those bought even in the best confectionery outlets at the too-competitive price of 30—40 pence. Their product costs more. All agree, however, that the meat should not have been pre-cooked. Even when minced meat is used — a very un-Cornish procedure — the mince must be raw.

Mavis's Cornish Pasty

The following recipe is the one Mavis follows, handed down from her mother; and she bakes half a dozen some weeks. She says she uses:

For the Filling: 50 g (2 oz) skirt of beef for each pasty but when she feels extravagant she increases the amount of beef to 75 g (3 oz). Like all of us, she looks back wistfully to the time when real rump steak was the usual filling.

For the Pastry: 450 g (1 lb) flour to 150 g (6 oz) lard and margarine mixed.

Her secret is to rub the fat in roughly (and not into 'small crumbs' as often advocated), roll it out and cut round a side-plate for guidance. She follows the side crimping school.

Method of Filling: Place on one half of the rolled-out dough a layer of thinly sliced turnip, then a layer of thinly sliced potatoes, adding sliced onion, if liked, and seasoning each layer with salt and pepper. Next comes the meat, cut up in small cubes with a sprinkling of flour, then a top layer of potatoes, to keep the meat moist. Glaze if desired. Bake in a hot oven at first, then reduce the heat for the one hour's baking.

Patty's Pasty

The following are required to make two pasties:

For the Shortcrust Pastry: 225 g (8 oz) flour, 100 g (4 oz) margarine and vegetable shortening mixed, ½ teaspoon salt.

For the Filling: 225 g (8 oz) chuck steak or 'pasty beef', 2 medium potatoes, a small swede (the Cornish call it turnip), 1 medium onion, salt and pepper.

Roll out pastry into two rounds, guided by a side-plate. Put the potatoes, sliced thinly and turnip, diced, in the pastry centres and dust over salt and pepper. Cut meat into small pieces and place on top of the vegetables. Top with the chopped onion. Sprinkle a teaspoon of flour over the top and season again. Dot with small pieces of butter. Damp the edges of the pasty and bring together on top, crimping with the fingers. Make a small slit either side of the top to allow the steam to escape, and brush with egg and milk. Bake at 232°C (450°F) for 20 minutes and then at 149°C (300°F) for a further 40 minutes.

Cousin Jack's Mutton Pasties

450 g (1 lb) mutton cut up small, 75 g (3 oz) potatoes, 50 g (2 oz) carrots, ½ onion (grated), salt and pepper, parsley to taste, pastry for pasties.

Knead pastry, divide into six pieces. Roll each piece into a circle the size of a large saucer. Mix all the other ingredients together and place on the circles of thin pastry. Turn the pastry over to make pasty shape and seal with milk or water. Prick all over, glaze with milk or egg and bake in a hot oven for the first 10 minutes, then reduce to a moderate oven for ¾—1 hour.

Minced Meat Pasties

For some reason children seem to prefer this un-Cornish variety and the mince itself may be made very tasty — and economical — by following the recipe for mince in the Meat section of this book. Many a mother has found that any scraps the children leave they will wolf up the next day in a pasty. As for the aesthetic risk of eating somebody else's left-overs, it is conveniently side-tracked by the old custom of putting the initials on the pasty. The origin of this custom was to ensure that the owner of the pasty could finish it at some future time, if necessary. You started eating from the uninitialled end.

A modern touch, for conveying a message on a pasty, is to paint it on with undiluted food colouring; such as 'Happy Christmas' or 'Birthday' or such, with the name of the honoured one.

Ham and Spinach Pasty

Look out for ham pieces sold cheaply in some supermarkets. Combine the finely chopped ham with an equal quantity of puréed spinach and blend with a little top milk or cream for moistness. Season with a grating of nutmeg, salt and pepper. Make pasties from some squares of pastry, crimping each at the top. Glaze by brushing with egg and milk. Bake as usual.

Leeky Pasties

Wash the leeks and trim them, cutting off the outer skins if not young enough. Drain them well and slice into lengths about the size of the pasties, adjusting the number of slices to fill each pasty. Season with pepper and salt. Bake as usual.

Fruit Pasties

Apple has always been a favourite filling, solo or married to blackberry, plum or other fruit in season. Apricots, fresh, canned, or dried and stewed, are very good combined with a little apricot jam. The idea of mixing fresh fruit with jam works out very well. All of the fruit pasties were served with dollops of cream, although today Cornish people are learning to cut down on it.

The Future

The pasty is a cheap, tasty and nourishing meal for all ages, needing no artificial aids in the eating — only fingers. If properly cooked it can be eaten hot or cold, requiring no sauces or side dishes. It is a rival to fish 'n chips, hamburgers and sandwiches, open, or 'giant' or otherwise. Maybe some enterprising Cornish couple will start a chain of pasty places more than just 'finger lickin' good, centered here with franchise outlets in Britain — and the world. Pasty places could work on the same principle as the USA pizza stores where you choose one of a score of fillings and watch TV for a few minutes until your choice is baked to a turn.

SAVOURY PIES AND TARTS

In folklore of all countries pies pop up all over the place. People talk about pies as often as they ate them, it seems. Why were they such a talking point? Was it because they were a kind of guessing game, as you never quite knew what was in a pie until it was opened? In mediaeval times all kinds of things might fly out of a pie, from a live creature to a parchment document your host might expect you to sign. Pies were fun.

The pie was, of course, the parent of the pasty. To intrigue, if not to whet the appetite, here are a few of our truly Cornish pies.

There was the Taddago pie, for instance, made from premature 'veers' or piglets. Muggety pie could contain any form of offal, or what the Americans deicately term 'variety meats'; anything from the cord of a calf, the intestines of a pig or sheep's pluck. The entrails of pigs, sheep and calves were well seasoned with herbs as were the lammy pies made from stillborn lambs. Old-time giblet pies had sugar and figges (raisins) and apple added. Squab pies there were a-plenty. But before giving recipes for meat and vegetable pies acceptable today, let us start, appropriately, with those featuring fish.

Fish Pies

The stargazy pies that haunt our old cook books with fishy eyes staring up to heaven knows what, are only talked about today. They were enjoyed at a time when no one minded seeing the animal cooked to look as if it might be alive, as was done with rabbit, hare, boar's head, peacocks, and other creatures in the fashion of past ·ages. Yet there was a cooking strategy in placing the heads upwards in the pies, if not necessarily in the tails perking upwards too. The nourishing oil from the brain drained into the body part to enrich the fish. (So much of what we buy is wasted today.)

Although it is unlikely we shall be called upon to create a stargazy pie now, here is a recipe contributed by the Boscastle branch from that oft quoted recipe book published by the *Cornwall Federation of Women's Institutes* of the early twenties.

Star-gazing Pie

Required: pastry, fish (6 or more pilchards preferably), pepper and salt, 2 or 3 hard-boiled eggs, if liked.

Prepare pastry, put the pilchards in pie-dish whole, and with heads left on, well season with pepper and salt, add eggs, cut in slices, lay pastry over and put the mouths of the pilchards through the pastry so that they can be seen (hence the name).

Fish and Oyster Pie

To make a few cooked oysters go farther they may be mixed with any cooked fish. Make a seasoning of breadcrumbs, pepper, salt, nutmeg and parsley chopped finely. Put into a pie-dish neat pieces of cooked fish, free of skin and bones. Sprinkle well with pepper and salt. On top of the fish place the oysters with the breadcrumbs. Fill up the dish with alternate layers of fish, oysters and seasoning. Pour over melted butter added to the juice from cooking the oysters. Cover with bars of puff pastry painted with egg yolk and milk and put into a quick oven until pastry is lightly browned.

Trout Pye (dated 1748)

Clean, wash and scale them, lard them with pieces of a Silver Eel rolled up in Spice and sweet Herbs, and Bay Leaves powder'd; lay on and between them the bottoms of slic'd Artichokes, Mushrooms, Oysters, Capers and slic'd Lemon; lay on Butter, and close the Pye.

Seafood Flan

This Breton cousin to a quiche may be made with a simple pastry or scone dough base and less cream in the sauce. But the original recipe requires a baked puff pastry case, with an assortment of seafood cooked and cut up as each type requires: oysters, mussels, winkles, lobster or crab. Some boiled mushrooms are sliced and added. The rich seafood sauce poured over this is made by reducing a fumet (essence) of fish stock to which has been added a few spoons of the water the mushrooms have been boiled in. After straining and seasoning 3 tablespoons of butter and 4 tablespoons of thick cream are added. The top of the flan is sprinkled with toasted breadcrumbs and melted butter, then browned under the grill. Some chefs add wine or lemon juice to the sauce when it has thickened.

Easy Pies

Packaged soups such as mushroom, celery or asparagus transform left-over fish pieces into a tasty pie. Use half the liquid mentioned but otherwise follow the directions; pour over the flaked fish in an oven-proof pie dish, add a knob of butter or tablespoon of cream. Top with a potato-mash crust. By the time the crust is light brown the pie will be ready to serve.

Herbs for Fish Pies

Herbs that enhance the flavour of fish pies are: marjoram, sage, parsley, rosemary and thyme. Spices include mace, nutmeg and paprika. Celery and garlic salts should be used with discretion.

Steak and Kidney Pies

Old fashioned steak and kidney pies are still made in some farmhouses with a large dumpling on the top instead of pastry. Here is a basic recipe for the filling for both types of pie.

Dumpling: For a suet dumpling, mix 75g (3 oz) grated suet (or dripping) with two cups self-raising flour, a pinch of salt and sufficient water to make a good dough. For a richer dumpling mix ½ cup milk with 3 well-beaten eggs and a pinch of salt, adding sufficient flour to make a stiff mixture. Spoon the dumpling over the simmering meat and stock, and keep well covered (without peeping) for 30 minutes. The dumpling cover for the pie is not added until 30 minutes before the steak and kidney stew is ready to serve.

The Meat Filling: Cube 670 g (1½ lb) beef and ½ ox kidney after removing membrane. Roll in seasoned flour and lightly brown in a little hot fat. Put in saucepan with boiling stock, a chopped onion, peppercorns and bay leaf. Cover with lid and simmer very gently for 1½ hours. If liked, 20 minutes before serving, raise heat a little, add one big dumpling or puff pastry.

Method for Pastry Pie: Prepare steak and kidney pie as described above. When cooked cool and place with some of its liquid in a pie-dish with a funnel or egg cup in centre. Taste for seasoning. Cover with puff pastry, slashing at each side of top to allow steam to escape. Brush with beaten egg and bake in a hot oven until pastry is lightly browned and cooked through. As the pie should have plenty of gravy when served it is a good idea to thicken some of the liquid left over when the steak and kidney was cooked and lift up a side of the crust and pour it in.

Pork Pie

This is eaten cold and for that reason must be made with hot water pastry.

The Pastry: 566 g (1¼ lb) flour, 225 g (½ lb) lard, ½ cup water, teaspoon salt.

Method: Mix flour and salt. Boil lard and water and add slowly to the flour, stirring continuously until well mixed. Use your hands as soon as the mixture is cool enough to handle. Roll out to 1·25 cm (½″) thick and form the pastry round a wooden cylinder about 17·5 cm (7″) in diameter and half as high, keeping enough in reserve to form a lid. If made in a tin mould, shape pastry smoothly round mould then fill with the meat mixture, pushing down well to firm it. Put on lid of pastry and pinch edges together. Slash pastry in the middle of the lid. Pin some brown paper round the pie, brush with beaten egg and bake in a moderate oven for 2½ hours. When the pie is baked and removed from the oven, pour the liquid in which the bones were stewed through the holes in the lid to form a jelly on top. Cool until this liquid sets into a jelly.

Meat filling for Pork Pie. This may be made the day before as it takes three hours to simmer. Cut 225 g (8 oz) pork from the bones. Cover bones with water and simmer for 3 hours. This should form a jelly when cold. Cut the pork into small cubes, trim off most of the fat. (Do not mince the meat.) Mix 5 tablespoons stock from the bone liquid with the meat and season well with salt and pepper, adding a pinch each of mace and ground ginger. Now put in the pie as described above.

Squab Pie

Traditionally made from a young pigeon or cormorant, as available, squab pie might be topped with apple, bacon bits, onions and scraps of mutton. But a still usable recipe for this pie dispenses with the bird. Here it is:

225 g (½ lb) mutton (fresh or minced), 450 g (1 lb) apples, 100 g (¼ lb) raisins, small onion, sugar and spice to taste, salt and pepper.

Dice meat and apples. Slice onion. Mix in other ingredients and season. Place in pie-dish with a little water and cover with pastry.

Apple and Onion Pie

This farmhouse vegetarian pie was served hot at high tea in the old days. The ingredients were:

Potatoes, apples, onions, salt, pepper, mace, nutmeg, butter, cider and puff pastry.

The raw peeled potatoes were thinly sliced and placed in a layer at the bottom of the pie-dish. These were covered with a layer of sliced onion, seasoned well and covered with a layer of peeled sliced apples. The layers were continued and the onion seasoned well until the dish was full. The top was dotted with butter and about 3 tablespoons of cider added. After covering with pastry the pie was baked in a moderate oven for about one hour.

Chicken Parsley Pie

Parsley was used profusely in our old-time cookery and because of its well known blood-cleansing properties is popular in Cornwall today. A favourite pie consisted of layers of seasoned chicken joints interspersed with thick layers of parsley, all drenched in well flavoured chicken stock. When baked one recipe instructs to open the top of the crust and pour in thick hot cream before serving.

Likky Pie

It is said this was a favourite with the Cornish saints who abjured meat.

900 g (2 lb) leeks, after cleaning are chopped into ½" lengths and are boiled until tender then strained and put into a pie-dish with the following: 50 g (2 oz) streaky bacon cut finely with scissors, 100 g (4 oz) cream, 2 well-beaten eggs and pepper and salt to taste. Cover with a good pastry and bake in a quick oven for about half an hour. In the old days this was served with clotted cream.

The Pious Touch

The saints likky pie omitted the bacon and had an undercrust as well as a top crust. The top crust was opened (just as was done with some pasties) and a whole egg was dropped into the steaming contents.

Rabbit Pie

Rabbit 'provides a feast for the countryman and labourer' records an old writer, 'its appetising aroma pervades farmhouse and cottage alike.'

Rabbit pie can be made in similar ways to chicken pies, as recipes are interchangeable with chicken. But the following found in a very old cookbook tickles my fancy. As you see, it extends a small rabbit by any other meat to hand.

Put into the bottom of a baking dish a few slices of ham or beef, cut the rabbit into as many pieces as required, season each bit with salt, pepper and pounded spices and arrange the rabbit joints and flesh in the dish as closely as possible. Add a glassful of broth if you have any, and if not a little white wine and water. Cover the pie-dish closely with a good crust and beat an egg in a gallipot and paint this over the top. Bake in a moderate oven for an hour and a half. Serve hot. But if the pie is to be eaten cold remember that it must be more highly seasoned.

The above is sound advice for all foods to be frozen or served cold, as every good cook knows!

The popular game pies of the gentry and richer farmers used venison as well as all those wild fowl in the shooting calendar.

Venison Pie

As usual, old cookbooks confuse pasty and pie and the following recipe for a venison pie from *Cassell's Dictionary of Cookery* labels this pie a pasty. But as we know a pasty doesn't include gravy and a pie must have gravy and that is why the stockpot and liquid made with the bones and carcass of the animal is so important when making a pie. Game pies follow that principle and are always best when not too highly 'herbed' as the aim is to preserve the true gamey flavour. This is particularly true of venison, although a little port wine, lemon juice and nutmeg were used for flavour, garlic and onion as well.

Venison 'Pasty' Pie

If the meat is fresh keep it for a fortnight or 3 weeks. Cut into pieces, simmer it well and make a good gravy from the liquid. Season with pepper, salt, port wine, vinegar and a little sugar. If too dry add a little fat mutton. Allow to get cold, then pack it in to the dish as closely as you can pack it with some of the gravy. Cover with pastry and put into oven. Serve balance of gravy at table.

Herby Pie

Meat was scarce in the case of the poor and even on the farms where the stock had to be turned into money to pay taxes. But we Cornish made the most of our vegetables and herbs — all 'for free'. Herby pie contained nettles, pepper-grass, parsley, mustard and spinach and sometimes had a few pieces of pork thrown in to make a better meal.

The Pig Pie Man.

Tom, Tom, the piper's son,
Stole a pig and away he run;
The pig was eat
And Tom was beat,
And Tom went howling down the street.

The 'pig' in the rhyme was not a live one, but a sweetmeat made of pastry with currants inside and two currants for eyes. (See opposite page).

84

SWEET TARTS AND PIES

Delving into Cornish history in search of our food my discovered heroine is not a saint but a wellbred woman of 36 summers who had the guts to cross the Tamar by ferry and then ride down the tortuous paths of our coastline, discovering Cornwall. Her name was Celia Fiennes and the year is judged to be 1698. In the fashion of her day she rode side-saddle. Having noticed Greek peasants, men as well as women, riding this way on their donkeys to slide off at danger points, and not fall head first over the animal's ears, perhaps this mode of riding was her salvation. Her horse did stumble in one of the potholed lanes and fell, but she seemed to survive the 'long miles' as she decribes them, and what is nearest our heart, she pays tribute to Cornish cooking and in particular to an apple tart. She was staying at the White Hart Inn at St Austell and described the tart thus:

'It's an apple pye with custard all on the top, it's the most acceptable entertainment that could be made for me; they scald their cream and milk . . . . and so it's a sort of clouted creame as we call it, with a little sugar, and so put on top of the apple pie.'

(For a few more details of this intrepid traveller see *Visitors to Cornwall by Ida Procter*, Dyllansow Truran-Cornish Publications.)

The type of tart blanketed in clotted cream that Celia Fiennes enjoyed would probably have been made that very Cornish way, still practised by some villagers. The fruit is cooked in a soup plate or shallow dish then covered with pastry. When baked the pastry cover is removed and placed on a plate. Then the fruit is mixed with sugar and spread over the pastry, which is then decorated with clouted cream.

Spinach or Chervil Tart

This 18th century recipe gives ingredients as follows:

1 gallon spinach or wild chervil, 8 oz melted butter, 1 lb sugar, 3 lemons, puff pastry, cream, fine sugar.

Wash and shred the spinach finely, melt butter and pour over it. Add the lemon pulp with the grated rind of two lemons and the sugar. Put mixture into a tart pan and cover with pastry. When the pastry is light brown take off the pastry lid and turn it upside down. Spoon over the spinach filling, topping it with clouted cream.

Sweet pies or tarts (the words were interchangeable) have always been as popular as the savoury ones. Even Tom the piper's son who stole a pig 'and away he run' didn't steal a real pig at all as we well know. He was 'beat' for stealing and eating a sweetmeat because the hawker (pyeman) sold sweet 'pies' baked to look like little pigs. Pigs, playing such an important part in the life-line of the average countryman, survive in popular porcelain and pottery piggy banks in our gift shops everywhere. Unfortunately I have no recipe for a piggy sweetmeat, but it was probably made of sweet cake or pastry with currant eyes and delighted the children as much as candyfloss and ice cream do today.

Cherry Pie

The very name makes the mouth water; but alas the cherry orchards, once a blossoming feature down the road from Carkeel, seem to have shrunk to a solitary tree or two in a farmer's garden. That is why a friend, Joan Rapson, and I were surprised to see a Cherry Pie Festival advertised when last we visited the church at Botus Fleming. The merrymakers may have scrounged enough fresh cherries, but to be on the safe side here is a recipe using canned ones:

1 pastry shell (7″), 2 tablespoons sugar, 1 heaped tablespoon cornflour, pinch of salt, 450 g (1 lb) tin canned cherries, almond essence.

Strain cherries and use one cup of the syrup and bring to boil. Add cornflour which has been blended with a little cold water and stir continuously to avoid lumps. Boil for two minutes and remove from fire. Add ¼ teaspoon almond essence and leave to cool slightly, then pour mixture into pastry shell. Place cherries on top of this and leave until cold. Top with whipped cream if desired.

For Sweet Flan Pastry, sufficient for two tarts, one filled as above:

100 g (4 oz) sugar, 200 g (8 oz) butter, 225 g (9 oz) flour.

Add 1—2 tablespoons of iced water to the dough and roll smoothly to fit pan. Bake until barely brown.

If fresh cherries are available they may be used as a filling for a pie or tart, with a puff paste or 'crumb' shell. Poach the fresh cherries in a little sweetened water, stone them and reduce juice to a syrup, or thicken with a little cornflour or arrowroot, finishing with a glaze incorporating a few drops of kirsch or rum.

Val's Crumbly Apple Pie

Cream half a cup of sugar and one egg with 125 g (5 oz) margarine or butter and two tablespoons cooking oil. Blend in 2 cups of flour sifted with 2 teaspoons of baking powder, and ¼ teaspoon salt.

Pack into two flan dishes. Fill with sliced cooking apples, a few sultanas and a little grated nutmeg. Grate the dough over the top of the tart and bake.

Our Very Own Fruit Pies

There is no better pudding than that made from the blackberries and 'urts' (whortleberries or bilberries) picked in the hedgerows, and the gooseberries, apples and plums from one's own garden. Here in my village there survives the supreme joy of cooking what you have grown, the joy of giving and receiving home-grown produce.

Heavenly Pies

With a Meringue Base

Buy or make a meringue shell. Fill it with fresh raspberries or strawberries, supplementing the fresh fruit if necessary with the canned or frozen variety. To draw out the flavour of the fruit, heat it without allowing to boil with sugar to taste. Add a tablespoon of gelatine dissolved in fruit juice or hot water, then a dash of lemon juice or sherry. Cool until thick then fold in ½ cup of whipped cream. Pour into shell and chill.

THE DAIRY'S WHITE MEATS

Puddings

The basic protein food of our ancestors was what were called white meats or witsul; comprising 'raw' milk, cream, sour milk, skimmed milk and home-made cheeses. The expression reminds us of the use of the word meat for many things not meat, for example 'cider meat' in a further chapter. Raw milk, so named, was fresh milk.

Scalded Cream

Or Clouted

Good Queen Bess's sailors brought news of Cornish clouted cream to her court and Celia Fiennes remarked upon it when she enjoyed that apple 'pye' at St Austell, already referred to in the chapter about sweet pies. 'They scald their cream and milk so it is a sort of clouted cream as we call it with a little sugar and so put on top of the apple pye.'

The old spellings of clouted are given by Dorothy Hartley in her *Food in England* (Macdonald London) — clowtyd, clowted, clawted, and clotted. The origin of the name, she says, is disputed, 'but a "clout" is a thick patch, presumably of leather, since you have old shoes unclouted and the cream wrinkles up in thick leathery folds.' Cloutynge was also a wrapping.

Scalded Cream

The Good Old Way

The large earthenware pans with sloping sides, that you can see at the Old Kiln Museum in Truro, were used for standing the fresh milk in for 12 hours in summer and 24 hours in wintertime. When the cream had risen the pan was lifted on to the side of the stove and subjected to moderate heat all day but was never allowed to get near boiling point. Then the pan was carefully moved to a cool place for the night and the next day was skimmed by ladle or scallop shell. It was then layered into a serving dish or bowl for the table, ensuring that there was a crusty topping. Each farmwife had her own method. Some played safe by standing the pan of milk with its risen cream over a saucepan or into water which was then brought slowly to the boil to heat up the bowl's contents slowly but adequately. Another farmwife, who used the same type of earthenware pan with sloping side, told me she knew when the cream was ready when an impression formed similar to the base of the pan. And Marion tells me many used tin bowls and placed them on top of the copper, often over water; all depending, of course, on the heat below.

Clotted Cream Today

Separated cream is left to stand in an uncovered bowl overnight. Next day the bowl is set over a large pan of water and allowed to heat up slowly until a thick crust is formed. 'But always leave the cream in a cool place for 24 hours before serving,' advises Marion.

Unfortunately the demand today for Cornish cream — much of it is sent by post to other counties — has commercialised the old product almost out of recognition.

Cheeses

Soft cheeses, home-made by allowing sour milk to drip dry from a tree, are as traditional to Cornwall as elsewhere and still possible in their best texture if fresh, unpastuerised milk is used. Mixed with cream and herbs such cottage cheeses can form the basis of salad dressings and all manner of dips and snacks. As for hard cheeses, Nancy remembers a woman cheese-maker coming every so often to their farm with the rennet, moulds and expertise to create good hard cheeses. But where is a real Cornish hard cheese today? Mr Michael Green, of Truro's famous *Real Ale and Cheese Shop* introduced me to *Tregosel* cheese, a full fat hard cheese from goat's milk. Mrs Elizabeth Waite who makes it and who I interviewed at her home-factory at Indian Queens has a success story (already done on radio) worthy of several pages here. Suffice it to say, she is 100 per cent Cornish, as are her goats and the milk she buys and pasteurises. Her product, sold nationally, is yet another tribute to Cornish enterprise.

Butter or Marg?

By 1873 'butterine', as margarine was first called, was being imported from the United States to be shunned by all except the poor. In the 1920's vitamins were added to margarine to improve the diet of those who bought it. After the Second World War when butter was obtainable again, margarine (at 1/1 per ½ lb) was mixed with 10% butter to attract sales.

Today margarine, because of its variety, spreadability, price and attendant health propaganda, is ousting butter — with a loss to the farmer and our good taste. The facts, as explained by our professor in my university nutrition course, are that there is not all that difference between the quantity of saturated fat in butter and most margarines. The reason is that many margarines are based on coconut and palm oils, actually among the few saturated oils of the vegetable world. This is why 'health' oils, such as sunflower seed oil, are gaining popularity as well as the soft margarines made from them.

Good butter, natural to good cooking in the past, is still considered essential in many dishes — even if cut by half, which should apply to all fats today, of whatever origin. Mixed with cooking oil, butter is the perfect medium for frying or brushing over meats and vegetables. What is a jacket potato or corn on the cob without butter? (Granted Americans use, to even better advantage, sour cream with their potatoes!) But true Cornish butter cannot be bettered.

Let's Discard the Ballyhoo

When it comes to diet and right living there is an awful lot of ballyhoo, all too obvious to those who study the subject. Take the cholesterol scare, for example: Sensible wives today send their husbands for a cholesterol level test and do not deny them a scraping of good butter on their bread — **neither do they cook with fats or deep fry anymore!**

Hard cheeses and that traditional pudding, junket, required rennet.

Rennet

16th Century Recipe

Let the calf suck as much as he will, just before he is killed, then take the milk bag out of the calf and let it lie 12 hours covered with stinging nettles till it is red. Then take out your curd and wash the bag clean and salt it inside and out and let it lie in salt for 24 hours. Wash your curd in new milk and clean it and put it back in the bag with 3 or 4 streakings (the last milk from the cow), a beaten egg or so, 12 cloves, a blade of mace, and skewer the bag shut and hang it in a pot. In another pot put ½ pint of salted water, 6 tops of the reddish blackthorn, as many of burnet, and 2 of sweet majoram and boil all together and let it cool, and put some of this flavoured water into the bag with the egg and thick milk and let the bag soak in the rest of it. This in which the bag lies (and into which the heavier liquid from inside the bag exudes) is the rennet, and so strong that the bag can be refilled and left to exude more than 6 or 7 times before the curdling action of the stomachic juice is exhausted.

Junket Today

With Pasteurised Milk

If you are exhausted even by reading the above, you will be thankful for the chemist's skill in giving us a rennet that will cope with pasteurised milk, as in the following recipe using a rennet essence that I now use regularly with success.

Warm 600 ml (1 pint) of fresh milk as supplied by your milkman, with one tablespoon of sugar (I use castor) to blood heat, add a teaspoon of *Little Miss Moffat Rennet Essence* and stir for a few seconds. Pour into a **warmed** dessert dish (or individual bowls) and allow to set for about 20 minutes. I place mine in the warming cupboard. Sprinkle with freshly grated nutmeg and serve. A few drops of almond or rum flavouring may be used, but some prefer the plain junket with that inimitable taste of good Cornish milk. Our traditional way of serving junket was with clotted cream and orchard fruits as in season.

Almond Cream

Pudding and Ingredients

This almond milk or almond cream mentioned in old recipes has tricked many into thinking it must be the milk or 'oil' of almonds.

Nonsense. It is a kind of milk pudding or almond custard and is used as an ingredient in certain recipes. Almond puddings, often use bitter and sweet almonds, mixed, for best flavour. One such is almond cream, but in this case using only sweet almonds:

250 g (½ lb) almonds were peeled and crushed in a mortar with 250 g (½ lb) castor sugar until a smooth paste. A cream was then made with 1·8 litres (3 pints) milk, 50 g (2 oz) flour and a few drops of vanilla essence. When cool the almond paste was folded in.

Milk Puddings

In Luxury Class

Tapioca, semolina, rice and macaroni puddings, using fresh milk and sometimes an egg or two, have always had a following of old people here and today the excellent tinned creamy milk puddings are a boon to those who cannot, or have no time to cook, or cannot afford that luxury of today — too much electricity or gas. Whether home-made or bought, anyone with a grill can lift a milk pudding into gourmet class by spreading a layer of jam over the top and then topping well to the edge with a fluffy meringue made from one or two egg whites with a tablespoon castor sugar. Lightly brown under the grill. The egg yolks may be incorporated in the body of the pudding.

Gran's Boiled Puddings

I remember my mother telling me that her mother swore she couldn't have brought the family of ten up without boiled puddings. Into these went every scrap of left-over bread, biscuit and cake crumbs. This easiest of all recipes required:

A cup each of finely shredded suet, grated breadcrumbs and washed currants. Mix with 2 tablespoons sugar, a little grated nutmeg, a teaspoon of grated lemon peel and a pinch of salt. When the dry ingredients are well mixed, work in 2 well-beaten eggs and ½ cup milk.

Wring out some small cloths in hot water, flour them and tie in each a small teacup amount of the mixture. Plunge puddings into a pot of boiling water and boil quickly. Turn them out on a hot dish, sprinkle with sugar or dribble golden syrup over and serve. Sometimes she made a large pudding instead of the individual ones. When available saffron was added for colour and flavour.

JUST DESSERTS

Desserts and sweets under the snob menu term of 'puddings' may be anything from an ice to a real pud or fruit salad. Topped with clotted cream our fruit dishes can be better than that of any other county or country. That is why it is a pity when they are prepared without knowledge. For example, the best cooks have never ever stewed first-class fruits. Stewing and baking are left only for the hard-textured second-class kinds.

Apples, pears, plums and apricots should be sliced to the shape of the fruits, as is done for good fruit salad, and then poached in a pan with very little syrup. The lightly sugared syrup may consist of water, cider or wine with a little lemon juice to bring out the flavour of the fruit. Actually, as the object of all fruit dishes is to conserve the colour and full taste of the fruit I am not in favour of alcohol, such as sherry or rum, which often gives fruit a fermented bias; excellent as that may be, say, for spongy confections such as trifles, savarin and babas.

Fruit Fools

For these the fruit is not poached but puréed and if possible with no water or liquid at all. I find Bramley apples — so full of natural juice — are puréed to perfection if sliced, dipped in water, drained, then set over a moderate heat in a pan with a lid. In the case of soft fruits such as strawberries, raspberries and blackberries the fruit for fools need hardly be cooked, merely heated, strained of pips, and then sweetened; then whipped cream and/or beaten white of egg (or custard) folded in. A good example is Apple Fool made with grated raw apple and a little lemon juice, sweetened with castor sugar, with or without cinnamon and folded into stiffly beaten white of egg and/or whipped cream, or custard.

Gooseberry Fool

Gooseberries, wild or garden grown, are still a favourite with the truly Cornish. (Mavis has been planting new bushes in her garden as I write this.)

Top and tail 450 g (1 lb) gooseberries and boil with 670 g (1½ lb) sugar and a cup of water. When the berries are soft press them through a sieve and mix with them, very gradually, a pint of milk or cream, or half milk and half cream. Serve cold.

Bilberries, known as urts here, were culled from hedgerows and eaten with clotted cream and sugar. Strained of pips they are excellent in a fool.

Rhubarb

Very Traditional

'What are those tall funnels for?' I asked Mrs Iris Rowse during my visit to Truro's fascinating old Kiln Museum on Chapel Hill. 'They look rather like miniature chimneys?' She told me they were for forcing rhubarb and eagerly sought in our very rhubarb-conscious county.

Crab Apples

Wild crab apples, Richard Mabey informs us, are the origin of the manifold varieties of apple in cultivation. As they have been used since antiquity, I presume that Eve tempted Adam with that very small one — the first crab apple!

A Blackberry Dessert

Uncooked

Selected from many blackberry recipes I give the following because I truly do believe in the preservation of vitamin content by not cooking, if possible.

Fill a flour bag with blackberries and, wearing rubber gloves, press the bag over a bowl until the rich black juice is fully extracted. Don't add sugar or anything to this thick juice. Just leave it in a warm room for a few hours to set. The consistency is that of junket. Serve with clotted cream.

Mulberries may be used as raspberries in various sweets. The fruit is ripe when it falls — hopefully, on grass.

Frosted Flowers

Fruit and Leaves

Small sprigs (such as mint) petals and sprays of tiny flowers make a delightful edible table decoration when frosted. Pick the flowers fresh, do not wash them but brush with a fine brush. Using an artist's paint brush, lightly coat the petals with egg white mixed with a tablespoon of white wine or cold water, taking care to cover the whole surface, not thickly but evenly. Now lay the flowers or petals in castor sugar, and sprinkle the sugar lightly over each flower until it is evenly coated. Lay the sugared flowers on a tray and allow them to dry naturally in a dry airy place or a 'cool' oven. When the flowers are crisp and dry leave for 2 or 3 days before storing. For fruits, follow the same method as above, choosing small fruits such as grapes and berries. Naturally, use only edible flowers and berries.

Ices

Alas, many of my delectable hedge and orchard fruit recipes, so typical of Cornwall, must find space in a further book. This limitation also applies to ice creams. Yet so intrigued am I at the ice holes providing ice for the gentry's sorbets, here is a brief reference to a tantalising subject.

As we all know, in olden times many a great house boasted its own ice hole. In the grounds of Golden Manor, near here in Roseland, there is a hole but a few feet deep, strongly suspected of having been used for storing ice. As I looked down the ornamentally bricked shaft I couldn't help wondering where the ice came from. The climate is so mild hereabouts one could not depend on the winter producing frost and ice. Then Mr Laurence O'Toole (author of that informative book, *The Roseland between River and Sea*) reminded me that waterways and ships, in place of the present roads and cars, brought supplies from other countries — of necessities and luxuries. In turn, this reminded me of the fact that ships sometimes used ice as ballast. To quote from my book *Cookery in Southern Africa*:

'In the middle of the 19th century an ice house was built on the shores of Table Bay to store ice .... the ice blocks were those cut in North American rivers and used as ballast in American barques on their return down the cold Humboldt current to the Horn, and so to Cape Town; after taking seekers of gold and silver to America.'

As ice was actually brought to Southern Africa surely we must presume it was carried even more easily from northern ports here?

Sorbets, served between courses or with the roasts to cool the palate were similar to our sherbets or water ices but with liqueurs, rum or other spirits added.

Orange Sherbet

In Freezing Tray

Boil 1½ cups sugar and 1 cup water for 5 minutes. Soften 1 tablespoon gelatine in 2 tablespoons cold water. Dissolve in hot syrup (do not boil). Beat 2 egg whites stiff. Pour the syrup gradually into them, beating continuously. Add 2 cups strained orange juice and 3 tablespoons lemon juice. Fold in well and pour into freezing tray at coldest temperature. When sherbet is mushy and almost frozen remove to a chilled bowl and beat well. Return to refrigerator tray and freeze until firm.

Sorbet

Mint with Liqueur

Bring 3 cups water and 3 cups sugar to the boil and boil for 6 minutes. Allow to cool a little, then stir in the juice of 2 lemons and the grated rind of a lemon. Add ½ cup creme-de-menthe liqueur and mix well. Pour the mixture into a refrigerator tray and freeze until almost set. Transfer sorbet to a bowl and beat to break up crystals. Return to refrigerator tray and freeze until firm but not solid. Serve in sorbet glasses decorated with mint sprigs.

Honey and Almond Sundae

One family brick of vanilla ice cream, 1½ tablespoons butter, 40 g (1½ oz) almonds, blanched and sliced, 3 tablespoons honey, 3 tablespoons lemon juice, 4 wafer biscuits.

Melt the butter in a small saucepan over a low heat and carefully brown the almonds in it. Remove from the heat, add the honey and lemon juice, pour over the ice cream, and serve hot.

CAKES .... SAFFRON AND OTHERWISE

'Thy plants are an orchard of pomegranates, with pleasant fruits; camphire, with spikenard and saffron.'

Solomon's Song IV 13 14

Saffron

Stamens of Crocus sativus

'As dear as saffron,' people still say. It has always been among the costliest of spices right through the ages, used medicinally and as a dye, even before the Romans found it was excellent for curdling and colouring cheese. But the story that crops up again and again in Cornish cookery books about the Phoenicians introducing it to our pre-Celtic ancestors may or may not be believed.

'The streams of Lebanon' referred to in the verse following our quotation from the Bible above, may tickle the fancy of Cornish cooks all the more when we realise that Lebanon was identified with the Phoenicians. Imagination runs riot: we might try to prove the birth of our saffron and clotted cream here from the East. But let's try to come to our senses. Assess history, in its socialogical sense.

My observation of tribal people in Africa leads me to conjecture that if the Ancient Britons did flog their tin on Mount Ictis they were chiefly attracted by their buyers' glass and bronze implements and the brightly dyed clothes they wore — as dazzling as the sun the Britons worshipped.(The time of the Druids and their uses of herbal medicines had yet to come.) When we think of it, to the few stray members of the sophisticated civilisations of Egypt and, later, Greece and Rome, when they visited or settled here, we must have appeared little more than savages. The Phoenicians, who were eventually swallowed by the Hellenic and Persian cultures and spoke a semitic language unintelligible to the inhabitants of our remote peninsula, were primarily seafaring men. If they seized the chance of swigging fresh or sour milk or maybe metheglin wherever they landed I, for one, cannot see them passing on their home arts of clouting cream or immersing the stamens of *Crocus sativus* to make a medicinal tea. My own conclusion is that the many uses for saffron, introduced by the Romans in a random fashion were later nurtured by that fount of international cookery knowledge, the rich abbeys and monasteries, where, actually, the chef's tall cap was born.

But let's return from trying to explode these enduring — and somewhat endearing — myths to the exploding prices of saffron from the 16th to the 18th century in Britain.

As it is estimated it takes about 4,300 blossoms to prepare one single ounce (25 g) of usable saffron the prices vary extraordinarily. The reason must be attributed to the success or otherwise of a harvest always in demand. One household account records saffron bought in 1548 for 12s a pound to another of £4 a pound in 1666. My cousin Nancy remembers her mother telling her of how, as a child, she was sent to the village shop on her bicycle with a threepenny bit which was weighed against a dram of saffron, sufficient for a week's baking. Saffron could be compared with the cost of silver, as is shown in an account of 1717 when a silver salver to be presented to King George I was listed as costing £4 11s and the saffron to fill it as much as £1 6s 6d (from the leaflet *The Saffron Crocus*, Saffron Walden Museum).

Was saffron ever cultivated in Cornwall?

Although it was grown commercially all over England, and particularly in Essex for centuries, and it is recorded that Cornwall consumed about 20% of all produced, it is difficult to track down where and when it was grown here. Indeed the subject, like a few others in my Cornish homeland, has become slightly pixilated for me. Full of hope, following tip-offs of a saffron meadow at Gerrans and another at Feock and, having been led up many a garden path with rumours of saffron parks and gardens, I have come to the reluctant conclusion that the Cornish might call anything saffron that is bright yellow: fields of rape, mustard, buttercups, or whatever. And when you ask old farmers if they have seen or heard of anyone growing saffron the reply can be 'the climate baint no good — don't ee know?'

Yet at long last a few clues have come to light. In an article on Cornish Cooking in the *Cornish Year Book* (Bossiney 1982) that much loved writer the late Marika Hanbury Tenison, states with assurance, 'For a long time the Cornish grew their own saffron, near and around Stratton, picking and grading the tiny stems of crocuses by hand.' She gives no source of her information. But when I followed up her clue and wrote to Mr Roy Thorn, Curator of Bude Museum he replied to me as follows:

'There is reference to the growing of saffron in a privately published book by a Mrs C Hawkey in 1871, titled *Neota* in which Mrs Hawkey states '. . . while for culinary purposes there were to be found the angelica and caraway plants and the saffron crocus, within which blue petals was stored a supply of genuine saffron colouring for the manifold cakes and Revel buns for which Launcells was celebrated.'

Launcells is a hamlet or parish adjoining Stratton, and the above account, explains Mr Thorn, refers to Launcells' vicarage gardens.

Another indication of a true saffron field is given in a chapter of a book *Around the Fal* published in 1983 by Extra Mural Studies, Exeter University. The author, Miss KNM Bowring, told me that she had met someone in the Mylor district who had known of a field at Penryn at the turn of the century that was actually sold as a saffron field, and was considered the last in production in Cornwall. As the field was owned by a medical man, she thought that the story has some credence.

And who really knows how the stamen of a certain crocus was discovered by the ancients for medicine, or why after its centuries' old use in Britain it got trapped for good in Cornish cakes? Thousands sold every week! Rather similar to my observation of the puzzling kiddley-wink derivation in the chapter *Soups and Pottages* this question, too, seems unanswerable. We Celts, with our colourful imagination, tend to merge myth and fact when we try to discover origins, and certainly one of the subjects that suffers most is food; as is indicated in other chapters. In the meantime, before we proceed with recipes and remedies using saffron, let's be warned. Because of its cost saffron was often faked and in the Middle Ages in some countries even the dealth penalty was imposed on those who sold it mixed with yellow substitutes. Just as with narcotic drugs today, saffron was suspect. The spurious saffron, adulterated in the last century by mixing pure saffron stamens with other plants such as *Carthamus tinctorius* — still cultivated in Spain for colouring soups and other dishes — was subject to tests as conscientious as those used by diamond dealers.

The grim suspicions surrounding the subject of saffron were even extended to its postal travels abroad. Knowing Johannesburg well and also the problems of the South African police (who have the unenviable job of judging the colour and morals of a polyglot population) I was amused to hear the following true story. In the early days of Cousin Jack's emigration to the Rand Mines, the nostrils of the Johannesburg Post Office sorters were assailed by certain letters from Cornwall, containing — what? On opening a letter for inspection the police decided the bright yellow contents must be rank poison. In time, however, they realised their mistake and allowed the fragrant parcels through, in increasing numbers as the immigrants from Cornwall swarmed in.

It was rather the same with the book *Black Beauty*, embargoed until someone discovered the heroine not to be a beautiful black girl but a horse. Strangely or significantly, neither the Cornish miners nor the Cape Malays (descended from Javanese slaves brought by Dutch East India Company ships in the 1660s) have introduced saffron into South African cookery. The Malays use turmeric (borrie) which, may be the colouring matter in some baker's saffron cakes in Cornwall today. But certainly not Blewetts — as I discovered when discussing the contentious subject with Mr Peter Blewett who heads the famous Truro confectionery shops established 1885. He assured me he spent hundreds of pounds monthly on saffron! He had found people are willing to pay more for cakes and buns with the true traditional flavour.

The home baker here, with justifiable pride, uses genuine saffron obtainable at Boots, in the form of fragile stamens priced — at the time of writing — at 85p for one-third of a gram.

Before I proceed with recipes, it is amusing to read that bees used to become intoxicated when they visited saffron fields but then, of course, they sucked from the stamens **neat**; while paradoxically, Pliny claimed that saffron 'allayed the fumes of wine and prevents drunkenness.' So Roman orgies were apparently relieved by the taking of saffron at table, to enable those who 'must' to go on drinking.

No such goings-on are reported concerning saffron consumption in Britain, although literary monks were acquainted with Homer's 'nepenthes', which they considered was attributable to the stamens of the *Crocus sativus*, and recorded its inordinately exhilarating effects. Yet the following recipe recommended in Cassell's *Dictionery of Cooking* (1896) for relieving indigestion depends on the exhilarating quality of alcohol, rather than that of saffron:

Add a pinch of saffron to a quarter of a pint of hot water, then infuse for 10 minutes. Stir in two or three tablespoons of brandy (or any other spirits) and add a lump of sugar. Serve hot or cold.

Among many old remedies which include saffron as an ingredient are cough mixtures for the consumptive. Even in my teenage days many suffered from the often fatal disease, which flourished in this moist climate. Today it has almost been eliminated, but not by saffron.

Saffron Cake

The original saffron cake has been described as more aromatic than sweet. It was moreover more bread than cake, perpetuating the confusion of the words in history that blamed King Alfred for burning the peasant woman's cakes — unleavened bread in fact — and of poor Marie Antoinette's words 'let them eat cake.' And anyway the French to this day are not clear cut about cakes, using words ranging from *gateau* to *patisserie*, and the English pronounced 'ploom cak'; best exampled in the French translation 'to sell like hot cakes' — *se vendre comme du pain frais* ('Pain', of course, being bread.)

An Old Recipe

Truly traditional saffron cake was made with yeast in the form of home-made barm or bought baker's yeast. The fat was sometimes butter, but more often lard or a mixture of both, while today margarine is sometimes used. An early 19th century recipe runs as follows:

Take a quartern (4 lb) of fine flour, a pound and a half of butter, three ounces of caraway seeds, six eggs well baten, a quarter of an ounce of cloves and mace fine beaten together, a little pounded cinnamon, a pound of sugar, a little rose-water and saffron, a pint and a half of yeast, and a quart of milk. Mix all together lightly in the folowing manner: First boil your milk and butter, then skim off the butter, and mix it with your flour, and a little of the milk. Stir the yeast into the rest (of the milk) and strain it. Mix it with the flour, put in your seeds and spice, rose-water, tincture of saffron, sugar and eggs. Beat it all well up, and bake it in a hoop or pan well buttered. Send it to a quick oven, and an hour and a half will do it.

NB: Those acquainted with bread and cake making may suspect the accuracy of the given proportion of liquid to flour.

Mavis's Saffron Cake

Today Mavis, my neighbour, says 'I daren't make more than one cake at a time because of the cost of the saffron.' (At time of writing each packet is 85 pence for one-third of a dram.) For her cake she uses the following ingredients. and her method may surprise some of you in some respects:

1 packet of saffron, 100 g (4 oz) lard and margarine mixed, 450 g (1 lb) flour, 75 g (3 oz) sugar, 25 g (1 oz) fresh yeast, ½ teaspoon salt.

Place the saffron to crispen (but not brown) in a 'cool' oven for a few minutes. Then crumble it into a teacup and cover with hot water. Leave to steep for two days. When you start to make your loaf rub the yeast in with the fat, crumbling it into the flour which has been sifted with the salt. (This yeast-crumbling trick she learnt from a baker.) Add the sugar and the currants and sultanas, as required. Now add the saffron water (unstrained) and enough water and milk to form a pliable dough. Knead the dough well and when it leaves the bowl and hands clean, place it in a plastic bag large enough to allow it to double its size. Put it in a warm place. Now grease well a 950 g (2 lb) bread tin and place the dough in it to rise again. Bake in a moderate oven for an hour. Turn out when cool.

NB: Genuine saffron cake contains the tiny stamen threads to declare their true origin.

Saffron Buns

Using the same recipes, buns were made from small to giant size, as still obtainable in profusion from confectioners in Truro, Falmouth and other centres today. Concerning the subject of buns, a neighbour tells me that her husband, newly arrived from the North Country and used to buttered tea-cakes, was somewhat nonplussed when he accepted an invitation to tea here and was presented with a large yellow bun, without butter.

As memories of my teenage holidays at Tregassick, Nancy's home, where fragrant saffron cake, clotted cream and delectable home-made jam were heaped greedily on to one plate, this introduction to a bun without butter needs an explanation. The offering of a saffron bun was a compliment if not a reward. For example, everyone who had helped with the harvest was given a huge saffron bun, munched hungrily in the fields or taken home to eat with the traditional clotted cream and preserves. Labourers 'living off the land' were usually far better fed than the miners, as is indicated in other chapters.

Nancy remembers as a child taking 'croust' to the fields, usually saffron buns and a flagon of cider; although her grandfather, she remembers insisted on his cold tea. Probably a Wesley man?

True Saffron

John Gerrard, the herbalist. described the saffron plant in his *Herball* (1597), thus:

The floure of Saffron doth first rise out of the ground nakedly in September, and in his long small grassie leaves shortly after, never bearing floure and leafe at once. The floure consisteth of six small blew leaves tending to purple, having in the middle many small yellow strings or threds, among which are two, three or more thick fat chives of a fierie colour somewhat reddish, of a strong smell when they be dried.

Bastard Saffron

French chefs, with an eagle eye for genuine saffron, tell us to beware of the bastard saffron that is redder in colour than the true one, which is a dark orange colour. Saffron was introduced into Spain by the Arabs and was cultivated in France from the 16th century. It is interesting to note that *curcuma*, an Indian plant whose yellowish rhizome, according to my *Larousse Gastronomique* smells of saffron and ginger, and has an 'acrid and bitter flavour', is used in curry powder and **English** mustard.

Traditional Heavy Cake (Hevva Cake)

The pilchard fever that set in with the huer's cries of 'Hevva hevva' up to the turn of the century, when enormous catches called 'celebration shoals' (hevvas) were landed often within the hour, demanded a quick celebration cake. Heavy Cake in its simplest oldest form was made as follows:

(1) 675 g (1½ lb) flour (well dried), 225 g (½ lb) currants (cleaned and washed), ½ teaspoon salt, clotted cream.

Make this into a paste with clotted cream and roll out until about an inch thick. Score the top for easy breaking after baking. Bake flat in a moderate oven until lightly brown on top.

(2) A popular recipe today is:

225 g (8 oz) flour, 50 g (2 oz) lard and the same quantity butter, 225 g (8 oz) mixed fruit (cleaned and dried), 50 g (2 oz) lemon peel, ½ teaspoon mixed spice, ¼ teaspoon ground nutmeg, 75 g (3 oz) castor sugar, 2 beaten eggs.

Mix all ingrdients well, with a little milk if necessary until of a stiff consistency. Roll out to about ½″ in thickness and bake in a flat greased tin for about half an hour.

Figgie Duff

For the following I am indebted to the Perranporth WI together with the delightful advertisement seen in a shop window about the early twenties.

Take a little suet, a little lard, a teaspoonful of baking powder. Rub this into ½ lb flour, add figs (raisins) to taste. Mix with cold milk or water to a stiff paste. Roll into 4″ squares about ½″ thick. Cut across the top and bake ½ hour.

Advertisement in shop window: *Figgy Duff 4d lb. More figgier 5d!*

Fairings

These traditional biscuits are far easier bought in packets, yet there is a certain satisfaction when you hand them round murmuring 'these are home-made.'

4 oz (100 g) flour, 1 teaspoon baking powder and 1 teaspoon each of bicarbonate of soda and ground ginger, ½ teaspoon mixed spice, a pinch salt, 50 g (2 oz) butter, 50 g (2 oz) castor sugar, 3 tablespoons of golden syrup.

Sift the dry ingredients, the flour, the baking powder, bicarbonate of soda, ground ginger, mixed spice and salt. Rub the butter into the flour until the mixture looks like breadcrumbs. Stir in the sugar.

Warm the golden syrup slightly, pouring it into a warm spoon and stir into the mixture to make a firm paste. Divide into two sausage-like rolls, cut into ¼″ slices. Place on a greased baking tray and bake in a hot oven for about 10 minutes.

Gingerbread

Oldest of All

That gingery spicy taste of fairings is indeed the taste of the oldest cake in the world, namely gingerbread. Actually the early Egyptians, Romans and German tribes baked gingerbread long before the Star of Bethlehem was noticed in the sky. The most famous gingerbread makers were monks in the monasteries who used wooden moulds carved into the likeness of flowers, animals and other objects and, most importantly, the heads of the famous. Indeed in those days a celebrity might feel he was missing out if his features were not cast in gingerbread; just as some politicians feel ignored today if not invited to appear on TV. At Queen Elizabeth's Court a special baker was employed to bake gingerbreads in honour of guests at special feasts. All were gilded for glamour, of course - hence the ominous old saying 'to take the gilt off the gingerbread.'

Here in Cornwall simple gingerbread was enjoyed by all for 'feasten' days, outside the gilded gentry; and after all who needs gold leaf when you've got clouted cream?

Old-fashioned Plate Gingerbread

When Honey is Plentiful

450 g (1 lb) honey, 150 g (6 oz) moist sugar, 25 g (1 oz) powdered cinnamon, 50 g (2 oz) candied lemon (cut into thin slices), 100 g (4 oz) sweet, blanched and sliced almonds, flour as required.

Melt honey in a saucepan, and when hot, mix all the other ingredients and sufficient flour to make it into a stiff paste. Roll the paste out two or three times, so as to have it quite smooth and stiff; make it into cakes of any shape or size, about ¼″ in thickness, and bake on buttered tins in a moderate oven for half-an-hour or more.

Gingerbread Sponge

This old recipe is more to modern taste than the old gingerbreads (or honey-cakes) which require molasses — for today's molasses can be too bitter. Although I'm told treacle can be obtained as an alternative, I play safe with syrup.

4 tablespoons melted butter, 250 g (½ lb) golden syrup, 375 g (¾ lb) cake flour, 4 tablespoons brown sugar, 15 g (½ oz) each ground ginger and mixed spice, 2 eggs, 1 teaspoon baking powder, milk if necessary.

Melt the butter with the syrup in a saucepan. Mix the flour, sugar, ginger and spices. Make a well in the middle of the mixture and pour in 2 well-beaten eggs. Add the warmed butter and syrup and baking powder. Mix thoroughly and if mixture is too stiff add a little milk, say, 1 tablespoon. Turn on to a well-greased baking tin and bake for 30 minutes at 180°C (350°F).

Gingerbread Boys Wear Jeans

Cut out gingerbread men from the cooked sponge as above with a tin cutter as obtainable, trim off any crumbs and decorate. Water and glacé icings are suitable for this, chopped nuts and tiny sweets may be used for decoration. A young mother anxious to be with-it for her 10-year-old twin boys birthday had the bright idea to make gingerbread men in jeans. 'But how can I get icing that denim colour?' I found out you mixed edible charcoal with a little Reckitts blue and a few drops of water and strain through muslin.

Natural Colours are Nicer

It is better to colour and flavour your own icings to get that special pastel glow of colour; a touch of Reckitts blue (dissolved) for pale blue icing; a touch of spinach juice for green, cochineal (or plum juice) for pink, etc. And there is nothing better than lemon juice, which reduces the sugariness and gives a creamy colour.

Chocolate Cake

Some claim that chocolate is an aphrodisiac and probably that is true, because chocolate cake is so popular with our menfolk. My dachshund Peggy, who lived until 17 years of age, was crazy about chocolate and my daughter-in-law's terrier copied the cat by jumping on the grand piano where Mistress had gift-wrapped a box of chocolates. But Cat wouldn't have torn apart the chocolate wrapping. Honours to cats.

Chocolate Cake

So Easy

1 tablespoon butter, 4 tablespoons water, 2 dessertspoons cocoa, 1 tablespoon golden syrup, 1 cup flour, 2 teaspoons baking powder, 3 eggs, salt, 1 teaspoon vanilla essence, 1 cup castor sugar.

Put water, butter, cocoa and syrup into a saucepan and dissolve slowly over low heat. Beat the eggs and sugar very well. Add half of the sifted flour, then the hot cocoa mixture, then the rest of the flour, baking powder, salt and vanilla essence. Bake in a moderate oven 180°C (350°F) for 18—20 minutes in two 20 cm (8″) layer tins. Cool on a wire rack.

For the Filling and Frosting: Cream 1¾ cups sifted icing sugar with ½ cup soft butter. Sift 2 tablespoons powdered milk with 1 tablespoon sifted cocoa and mix in to the butter and icing mixture. Flavour with liqueur or rum.

Sponge to the Rescue

For Tea or 'Afters'

There's nothing so timely as a sponge. You can buy one fairly cheaply and slice, fill and top with cream and pieces of canned fruit for tea or sweet. Or cut up into tiny cakes, icing each decoratively. Or make your own and do likewise. Sandwiched with jam and grated coconut, cut into fancy shapes and garnished with myrtle sprigs, thinly cut sponge sandwiches were known as Bermuda Witches.

Hot Milk Sponge

1 cup flour, 1 teaspoon baking powder, pinch salt, 2 eggs, vanilla essence, ¾ cup sugar, ½ cup hot milk and 2 tablespoons butter.

Sieve flour, baking powder and salt. Whisk eggs and sugar until stiff. Fold in dry ingredients and hot milk mixture alternately. Bake at 200°C (400°F) for about 25 minutes in tins. Sandwich with filling of your choice.

Christmas Fruit Cake

Fruit Boiled but Good

Boil together the following for 30 minutes:

500 ml (2 cups) water, 500 g (1 lb) each of raisins, currants, sultanas, sugar, 250 g (½ lb) butter.

Add the following chopped ingredients five minutes before the 30 minutes is up:

250 g (½ lb) each of candied peel, mixed nuts, dates, dried apricots, glacé cherries.

Remove from the stove and while still warm, mix in a heaped teaspoon of bicarbonate of soda. This will froth, but allow to cool and when quite cold add:

3 or 4 beaten eggs, 1 kg (2 lb) flour sifted with ½ teaspoon salt and 2 teaspoons baking powder. Lastly add 2 tablespoons brandy.

Line a 20 cm (8″) square (or equivalent) round tin with a double thickness of brown greased paper, extending above tin. Bake at 150°C (300°F) for one hour, reduce temperature to 130°C (250°F) for 2—3 hours. Test with skewer to be sure centre is not moist. Pierce and pour over more brandy. Wrap immediately in double layers of foil, allow to cool and keep wrapped in foil till ready for icing.

Fat-Free Fruitcake

Today's Speciality

1 cup sunflower oil, 1½ cups brown sugar, 4 eggs, 3 cups sifted flour, 1 cup thinly sliced citron or candied fruit, 1½ cups whole glacé cherries. 1 cup chopped glacé pineapple, 1 cup chopped glacé figs, 1 cup seedless raisins, 1 teaspoon baking powder, ¼ teaspoon salt, 2 teaspoons cinnamon, 2 teaspoons mixed spice, 1 teaspoon cloves, 1 cup orange juice.

Heat oven to 140°C (275°F). Line two 9″ x 5″ x 3″ pans with lightly greased greaseproof paper. Combine oil, sugar and eggs and beat for two minutes. In a large bowl, combine 1 cup flour with fruits. Sift remaining flour with baking flour, salt and spice. Stir into mixture alternatively with orange juice. Pour batter over fruit mixture; blend well. Turn into prepared pans. Place a pan of water on lower oven rack. Bake cakes for 2½—3 hours or until done. Cool on wire racks; remove from pans; peel off paper. Wrap in cloth dampened in wine or brandy, then in foil. Before serving, glaze top and decorate. Chill for each slicing.

For the Glaze: 2 tablespoons brown sugar, 1 tablespoon golden syrup, 2 tablespoons water.

Boil sugar, syrup and water. Simmer for two minutes. Brush over cake.

Variation: 3 cups coarsely chopped nuts may be added if cake is not required specifically fat-free.

Honey Loaf Cake
A Prize Winner

4 tablespoons butter, 8 tablespoons brown sugar, 2 eggs, 2 cups self-raising flour, ¼ teaspoon mixed spice, pinch of salt, 1 heaped tablespoon honey, 2 large bananas (mashed thoroughly), 10 tablespoons mixed sultanas, cherries and currants, 1 cup chopped walnuts.

Sieve together flour, salt and mixed spice. Cream butter and sugar well. Add lightly beaten eggs gradually, then add sieved mixture alternately with the honey and mashed bananas. Finally add the mixed fruit and walnuts. Mix well. Put mixture into a greased and double lined loaf tin (9″ x 5″). Cover top with sheet of greaseproof paper. Bake on the middle shelf at 180°C (350°F) for about 45 minutes and then reduce the heat to 155°C (310°F) for another 45 minutes. Delicious served sliced and spread with butter.

Pyskies for the Kids. Sponges made in castle pudding moulds are covered with white icing, features in coloured icing, non pareils at bottom, chocolate patties for feet and wigs of liquorice.

BREADS OF OLD AND OF TODAY

As mentioned elsewhere in this book the first breads were popularly called 'cake'. That old nursery rhyme *Pat a cake, pat a cake, baker's man* referred to bread, not cake as we know it, and the 'cross it with T' indicated the law's insistence on the baker's sign, the brand name; so that the loaf, good, bad or indifferent could be traced to its source. Good King Alfred did not burn the peasant woman's cake, but her bread — flat loaves laid on the embers of an open fire. When Marie Antoinette suggested that the hungry French peasants eat cake when they had no bread she was probably referring to unleavened bread known as *Kuchen* (cake) in her native Austria.

Throughout the ages the production of bread and cake has not only been leavened with laws, from grower through miller to middleman but also with fun. The baker's gingerbread men of the Middle Ages supplied the fun of the fair, gilded or not as may be. Corn, taxed through the ages, driving thousands of Cornish at times to emigrate, was subject to all kinds of supplementary growths when milled for flour. Strangest of all stories to me are those relating to the bulb of the poisonous wild arum lily and to pillas, a small yellow grain and both part of our past.

The farinaceous bulb of the very poisonous wild arum lily, known as Lords and Ladies, *Arum maculatum*, (which grows in the shade of the hedgerows and woods) when boiled loses its poison. It was then ground, and added to other grains for flour. The cooked ground roots of this bulb went under the name of Portland sago and was used as sago in puddings, while the powder was employed for a sort of salop, a common drink before the introduction of coffee houses in the 17th century.

Strange to tell, on my last visit to South Africa's Cape Province (1984) I came across a little book *Veldkos* (Hout Bay Museum) which included a reference to the prolific wild arum lily (*varkblom* — pig lily) said to be rooted out by porcupines and used in the past to feed pigs. More than that: the Hottentots made a bread from the root by boiling it in several waters, drying the bulbs in the sun, then roasting them in embers!

But the story I heard that I haven't been able to confirm is that the wild arum lily bulbs were collected here in Cornwall by women and children and after 'baking the poison out' were sent to the millers who ground them and added the powder to grain to serve as an edible ballast for ships in Falmouth harbour. I can understand the idea of having ballast that may be eaten in time of emergency, as some Japanese ships to this day carry edible seaweed for like purpose. But the whole subject presents so many questions for which I have found no answers that I leave you, the reader, to fill in the true facts — if you know them, or when you come across them.

Pillas

Before potatoes gradually took over as a simple diet for our Cornish poor from the 17th Century onwards, a certain grain, known as pillas, not unlike rye, was made into a nourishing 'gurt' (porridge). It was also used to supplement corn in bread and was added to potatoes for pig feed. Briefly, this small yellow grain was damped and placed in the chimney corner until it became 'cheeny' — showed signs of sprouting. It was then spread out on a 'baker' and roasted, then it was crushed and eaten as gurt with skimmed milk. It was also used to supplement flour in puddings. As sometimes it was added to strengthen a malt brew at the cheeny stage (before the drying) the harassed excisemen forbade the harassed housewives to put their grain 'to cheeny'. The women, feeling harassed in all respects anyway, deprived of something they had invented themselves, were furious. 'At the cheeny' the pillas must have made a good yeast.

Reading about the preparation of pillas intrigued me as at one stage, the cheeny, it seems to have had something in common with the making of *magou*, a porridge enjoyed by tribal Africans which in Lesotho (formerly Basutoland) is made from sprouted Kaffir corn (a variety of sorghum). Only a few years before writing this I saw women at the carpet weaving factory in the mountains of Lesotho enjoying their mid-day break spooning up the porridge they had brought with them. Looking closely at one bowl I saw quite distinctly tiny bubbles prancing. No wonder they were enjoying their 'tea break'! That yeasty porridge revived and nourished them, exceeding by far anything they might buy at the trading store.

All Grist to the Mill

The miller on the bank of every fast-flowing stream was seldom surprised at what he was expected to mill. All he cared about was his percentage of the flour he milled. They said that if you met an honest miller he'd have hair on the palm of his hands, but that's a farmer's story, always 'agin' the miller and his toll. A miller could tell by the feeling of the grain exactly how to set the grinding stones for milling flour. 'He had a thumb of gold parde' observed Chaucer; the millers thumb was a traditional asset as well as a pun on his thieving.

Bread in the past could consist of several mixed grains, plus peas, from the horsebread sometimes eaten by humans, to the refined wheaten loaf for feast days. True bread depended on a rising agent, initially a home-made leaven or barm made from hops or potatoes. Before my recipes for the yeasts of yesterday, here is just a word about those we buy today.

Yeasts Now

Today most home bakers use dried yeast, yet fresh yeast, if not in the old convenient yeast cake form, is still sold by the ounce in some supermarkets. (I get mine from Liptons in Truro.) The latest dried yeast which short-cuts the usual methods is Harvest Gold fermipan yeast which is mixed directly into the flour. The usual thing is to use half the quantity of dried yeast; 25 g (1 oz) fresh yeast equals 15 g (½ oz) of dried yeast, but with Harvest Gold you can use even less than half, so long as you lengthen the rising time of the dough.

Dried yeast likes a slightly higher temperature for reconstitution than fresh yeast does. Fresh yeast is usually dissolved in the liquid before adding it to the flour, whereas dried yeast is best sprinkled on the warm water or liquid in which some sugar has been dissolved. Leave it for 10 minutes, until the liquid froths up, then use as fresh yeast.

The leavens or yeasts of the past were always fresh (moist) yeasts. Actually making the yeast itself was a challenge, met as usual in those days by enterprising housewives. Among the many home-made yeasts in my collection are the following — one from a member of the Mullion WI and the other from a member of St Just WI.

Barley Bread

To make the Leaven mix a small quantity of barley flour with warm water into a dough. Form it into a round shape, like a pat of butter; make a dent in the centre with the thumb, about half-way through. Set the dough on a plate, cross it lightly twice, like a hot-cross bun, and fill the dent with warm water. Set it aside for a few days when the dough will have fermented and split like an over-ripe fruit. It is then ready for use instead of yeast to 'plum' the bread, which is mixed in the usual way with warm water and a little salt. When the bread has been sufficiently kneaded, take a small piece of the dough and prepare it for leaven against the next baking day. Cover the newly-mixed bread with a cloth and set in a warm place. When risen, form into cone-shaped loaves and bake under a kettle on the hearth. The loaves were usually grouped in three's and the soft crust, where the loaves touched each other, was called 'kissing crust'.

Barm

1 tablespoon of flour, a tablespoon of sugar, 1 potato, boiled and mashed.

Squeeze potato, flour and sugar together, then add warm water enough to make a good size bottleful; put three or four raisins in to make it ferment; cork bottle firmly, leave two or three days before using.

The Friendship Cake

Barm, yeast or leaven when initiated and bottled became a very personal possession, handed from one friend to another to start off her sponge. A revival of this old custom lives on in the Friendship Cake. A little leaven (called a plant) in a bottle, plus the recipe is going the rounds of our village at time of writing. As in the case of a chain letter the recipient is expected to follow the directions exactly, stirring the plant for two days, feeding it on the third (with flour, sugar and milk), stirring again on the 4th day, then dividing it into 3 pieces, 1 to keep, 1 to make and 1 to give away. Then the method of making the fruit cake follows.

It is said this latest friendship chain started off in Falmouth. Anyway the participator in the fruit cake plant thing ends up with the satisfaction of not having broken the chain (we Cornish are superstitious), with a fine fruity family cake and something to talk about other than the weather.

Easiest Brown Bread

Made from Wholemeal

The following using whole-wheat flour and not the usual half whole-wheat and half ordinary white, is very simple:

750 g (1½ lb) whole-meal flour, 1 sachet dried yeast (Harvest Gold Fermipan), 15 g (½ oz) lard, 400 ml (¾ pt) warm water, 2 level teaspoons salt, 1 level tablespoon brown sugar.

Mix flour, sugar and salt in large bowl. Rub in fat with fingertips. Add yeast, stirring thoroughly. Add liquid and beat together to form firm dough. Turn on to lightly floured surface and knead by folding dough towards you, then pushing away with palm of hand, until firm and elastic for about 10 minutes. Shape into a ball. Place in a large bowl covered with oiled polythene. Leave to rise until double in size — 1 to 2 hours. Uncover, knock back and knead. Bake at 230°C (450°F) for 20—25 minutes.

No one panicked in the old days at the prospect of holidays with bread in short supply. Of course most women made their own. The following recipe is from one of those supplied by the *Flour Advisory Bureau* (21 Arlington Street, London SW1A 1RN):

White Bread

This recipe makes about 2½ lb dough. Use for loaves and rolls.

Yeast liquid: Blend ½ oz fresh yeast into ¾ pint water or dissolve 1 level teaspoon sugar in ¾ pint warm water (110°F, 40°C), sprinkle on 2 level teaspoons dried yeast and leave until frothy, about 10 minutes. (For slightly enriched bread use milk and water mixed instead of water.)

Other ingredients: 1½ lb plain flour, 2 level teaspoons salt, 50 g (2 oz) lard or margarine.

Prepare yeast liquid. Mix flour and salt and rub in fat. Add yeast liquid and work to a firm dough until sides of bowl are clean. Turn dough onto a lightly floured surface and knead thoroughly until firm and elastic and no longer sticky. It will take about 10 minutes.

Shape dough into a ball and place in a large, lightly oiled polythene bag, tied loosely at the top. Leave to rise until dough is double size and springs back when pressed gently with a floured finger.

Rising times vary with temperature.

Quick rise: 45—60 minutes in a warm place.

Slower rise: 2 hours at average room temperature.

Cold rise: 12—24 hours in a refrigerator.

Return to room temperature before shaping. Turn risen dough onto a lightly floured surface, flatten with the knuckles to knock out the air bubbles, and knead until dough is firm, about 2 minutes. Shape and finish as required.

To prove place shaped dough in a large, lightly oiled polythene bag and leave until dough is double in size or rises to top of tin. It will take 30—40 minutes in a warm place, 1—1½ hours at room temperature, 12—24 hours in a refrigerator.

Remove from polythene bag and bake in a hot oven, 425°F (220°C).

A 2 lb loaf takes 45—50 minutes, 1 lb loaf takes 30—40 minutes, Crown loaf takes 30—35 minutes, Cob takes 30—40 minutes, Plait takes 30—35 minutes, Rolls take about 20 minutes.

Splits

Thunder and Lightning

Thunder and lightning is the name given to splits eaten with a spreading of treacle (golden syrup) or jam topped with clotted cream. The expression is attributed to the controversy of whether you should put the cream or the treacle on first. As we have always used cream here instead of butter on **cold** scones and splits it may reasonably be argued we Cornish prefer to turn turtle the usual procedure and top with the jam or treacle. Although to eat our words, in the case of treacle it can be better controlled if dripped on the split first before the cream. Much ado about nothing. But the splits **are** something:

Cream 15 g (½ oz) castor sugar with 15 g (½ oz) yeast until liquid. Add 250 ml (½ pint) of tepid milk. Sift 450 g (1 lb) flour and a teaspoon salt. Melt 25 g (1 oz) butter and add this with the milk and yeast to the flour, mixing all to a smooth dough. Leave to rise in a draught-free warm place for 45 minutes. Shape with the hands into balls and bake in a floured baking tin, in a hot oven 200°C (400°F) for about 20 minutes. Split and serve hot with butter, or leave until cold and serve with syrup or jam and clotted cream.

The Croissant

The French croissant is so popular that it is sold by most confectioners. But it doesn't come up to our standard, as eaten in France, where it is usually made with real butter; although the French scorn to serve butter **with** their croissants.

By referring to the diagrams given with our recipe you will find no difficulty in making the croissants, with a little practice, and yours will taste better than most of those to be bought — because you will use good butter.

450 g (8 oz) flour, 1 teaspoon sugar, ½ teaspoon salt, a little beaten egg for glazing, 1 dessertspoon dried yeast, 75—125 g (3—4 oz butter), 150 ml (¼ pint) milk (lukewarm).

Add 1 teaspoon sugar to 150 ml (¼ pint) lukewarm milk and sprinkle the dried yeast over the top. Allow to stand until the yeast becomes active. Then stir into the flour, mixing to a soft dough. Leave in a warm place to rise for 1 hour. Turn on to floured board and knead lightly. Roll dough out to an oblong strip.

Divide butter into three portions. *Cut one portion into small pieces and dot these over two-thirds of dough surface. Dredge slightly with flour, then fold up plain surface, covering half of butter-covered area, and fold top one-third down, making 3 folds. Turn pastry half round, fold to side and roll out again to a long strip.* Repeat process from * to * until all butter is incorporated. Roll out and fold once more, then press out paste thinly to a large circle. Divide into wedges from rounded side to point, and shape like a crescent with point to top. Leave in a warm place 15 minutes to prove. Brush over with beaten egg, sprinkle with poppy seeds (if liked) and bake in a hot oven 220°C (400°F) for about 15 minutes.

How to Shape the Croissant

Potato Bread or Cake

A Simple Recipe

While they are hot mash 225 g (8 oz) boiled potatoes with 15 g (½ oz) butter. Add salt, and 50 g (2 oz) flour, mixing all evenly. Roll out thinly on a floured board. Cut into saucer-sized rounds and place on a hot greased griddle or frypan. Prick with a fork and cook three minutes each side. Serve hot for tea, buttered, or as an accompaniment for meat.

Potato Cake

A Different Way

One cup grated raw peeled potato, 2 teaspoons lemon juice, 1 cup sifted flour, 1 cup mashed potatoes, 1 teaspoon salt, pepper, 2 teaspoons baking powder, 1 egg slightly beaten, 1 cup buttermilk, ¼ cup butter or margarine, melted.

In a small bowl, toss grated potato, with lemon juice to coat well. Put into cheesecloth; press to squeeze out as much liquid as possible. In large bowl, combine flour and mashed potatoes, beating well with spoon. Add raw potato to flour mixture along with salt and baking powder. Add egg and buttermilk, beating to mix well. Heat frying pan, add 2—3 tablespoons oil and drop in batter 1 tablespoon at a time. Cook until nicely brown and potato is cooked. Continue until batter is used. Serve hot, buttered, and sprinkled with sugar, for tea. Or serve as a potato substitute. Yield: about 20.

A Bite into History

But Never Your Plate

Trenchers or plates of early medieval times were made of dough baked hard and sliced into rectangles or circles as required. Your high position might earn you two or three plates but if you were below the salt and found yourself with only one it was allowable for you to break it neatly into two parts, to accommodate both meat and pud. But never, as every well-brought-up child knew, were you allowed to bite into your plate. The left-over trenchers soaked in gravy were handed down to the servants and from them to the poor. While these pages almost ignore the gentry because so much has already been written about them in other books, I cannot resist mentioning the following lordly practice.

It was frequently usual for a couple seated together to eat from one trencher, 'more particularly if the relations between them were of an intimate nature'. According to Walpole, as late as the middle of the last century, the old Duke and Duchess of Hamilton occupied the dias at the head of the dining-room and preserved the traditional manner of sharing the same plate — a token of attachment and a tender recollection of unreturnable youth. (There is no mention of second childhood.)

Bread Books

For those interested in making good bread a recommended book is *English Bread and Yeast Cookery, Elizabeth David (Penguin £3.50)*. It gives recipes for bread, new and old, and discusses yeast, flavourings and various flours.

Ways with Yeast produced by the home economics test kitchen of the Flour Advisory Bureau is an excellent book. The bureau, financed by the milling industry, also supplies leaflets on dieting and the making of snacks for school lunch boxes and home entertaining. The address is 21 Arlington Street, London SW1A 1RN.

OPEN HEARTH BAKING

When we see 'kettle' in an old recipe it is understood that it was not a 'tay-kettle' but a large iron three-legged pot that could be hung from the trivet for cooking, stood over the embers or inverted to cover bread and cakes when baking. The procedure is exactly described in the chapter *The Cottage Home, Cornish Homes and Customs*, by Mr EK Hamilton Jenkin ((JM Dent & Sons Ltd and David and Charles).

'Whenever baking had to be done the "brandis" or heavy iron trivet was first drawn forward into the centre of the hearth and on it was placed a round sheet of iron, known as the "baking ire". With the aid of the "fire-hook" which took the place on the open hearth of the poker in ordinary grates, the smouldering embers were raked round the brandis and under the baking iron and were fanned into flame with the "bellis" (bellows).

'As soon as the baking iron had been heated to the proper temperature it was taken off the brandis, carefully wiped and greased and replaced on the hearth. On to it the bread or other food was then laid and covered by the inverted kettle. Hot embers were raked around and a fire of furze and "bruss" (dried hedge gatherings, etc) built up over the whole. Beneath this the bread, protected from all dirt and ash, was left to cook for about an hour and a half, at the end of which time the embers were removed, the kettle lifted off and there was the loaf baked to perfection. All sorts of dishes appear to have been baked in this way, but sometimes a baker was used instead of the kettle; like a large frying pan without a handle it had no legs. The other important utensil, the crock for boiling was hung from a crossbar in the chimney or on the brandis and could be used if necessary and inverted over the baking iron instead of a kettle.'

A St Just member of the WI instructs about the baking iron and kettle. 'Heat baking iron to red heat. Heat kettle. Place bread or cake on iron, cover with kettle, surround with hot embers and cover with burning furze and turf. Bake 1—1½ hours according to size.'

Some old verse paying tribute to Mother's cooking runs as follows:

Seems now I see her clutten down,
The fire-ook in her haand
A-foochen' bout the burnen sticks
And doin' pasties graand'
And then she'd saay, They're ready, 'bleeve'!
Just as the fit wud taake her,
And slip a knife right in between
The Bake-ire and the baaker.

(Contributed by Mr Morgan Anthony in the Chapter *The Cottage Home, Cornish Homes and Customs.*)

Talking about knives, these old Cornish ways of cooking seem civilised. As bread was often baked in the ashes without tins, people were used to finding ash or pieces of charcoal encrusted in their loaves. Indeed on record is a Sixteenth Century school master's injunction at table, after he had said grace:

'Let every man draw his knife and chip his bread if there be any ashes or coles in the crust.' *Claude Hollybande, The Frency Lyttelton, 1593).* Yes, special permission for students to draw their knives it seems!

The old open hearth methods of cooking were supplemented by their invaluable cloam oven, especially, as a WI member wrote, 'for special once-a-week baking.' Some cloam ovens contained a smaller oven inside them. The oven was made red hot with a fire of sticks of furze and wood, when the remains of the fire were raked out. Tarts and cakes were placed in the smaller oven and bread under iron kettles in the larger. 'When closed the oven should not be opened until the time for the cooking is up. Our oven would take up to ten pans', reports a WI member from St Kea. And when I visited the fascinating Old Kiln Museum of Truro Pottery I noticed that on top of each cloam oven was scored not only a pimpled design (lost to sight when the oven was built in) but an indentation of sticks, acquainting the buyer with the number of loaves one might expect to bake in that particular size of oven. Wet cloths called 'dollys' were used for mopping up the ashes which, by creating steam, helped in the baking of good bread. Bakers kept a tin of boiling water in their ovens for the same purpose.

HONEY AND DRINKS

That Make the World Go Round

Oldest and most valued of all sweeteners is honey. And because too many foods have lost their mineral content pure honey is in much demand in most countries where purists seek it from sources they are sure are unadulterated.

Honey — Nectar of the Gods

Originally honey was produced from the apiaries run by the monasteries, required as it was in vast quantities for metheglin and mead. When the monasteries were closed by Henry VIII it was left to the gentry and yeomen and cottagers to produce their own honey and make their own mead. The output of honey collected commercially must have been considerable as Falmouth exported beeswax at one period. Later, when sugar was cheaper, golden syrup took over to such an extent that people today remember their parents' leg-pulling story of 'Cornish treacle mines'.

Honey supplies dwindled in Cornwall until the Second World War, when an incentive to keep bees again arose because of the Government's extra sugar ration for the bees' winter sustenance. Surviving today are the signs 'Honey for Sale', prevalent in some areas, which lure health-conscious visitors up country lanes, avid for pure Cornish honey at its source.

There is no need to give honey advice. So many have indulged in it, including 'Everest Hillary's father, a New Zealand bee-keeper who claimed Sir Edmund 'did it all on honey'; and that book of upteen editions from 1958 *Folk Medicine* by DC Jarvis MD who persuaded half the civilised world to try out cider vinegar and honey.

Honey was used even before salt as a preservative for keeping such foods as butter and herbs. Today one beekeeper's wife enjoys packing fresh mint, as her mother did, into left-over honey for keeping.

Even without fermentation honey was considered an aphrodisiac and seems respnsible for at least one tremendous feat, if we can credit a translated 16th century poem about an Arab hero. It was said he successfully made love to 80 virgins in one night and in all seriousness it was recorded his diet before he united with these was 'honey and milk and ripe pigeon peas'. Perhaps vegetarians have something to say here. Pulses plus honey — who needs meat?

Mead and Metheglin

Aphrodisiacs

Mead, metheglin or hydromel are the oldest alcoholic drinks on earth. Mead is certainly one of our oldest words and according to the *Concise Oxford Dictionary* it is rooted in the Indo-European tongue. It occurs in Dutch, Icelandic, Danish, Swedish, German, Irish, Lithuanian, Russian, Sanskrit, Zend, Modern Persian and Greek (methu). The Angles and Saxons brought mead into Briton and, it seems, took it to bed with them, including the honeymoon.

Metheglin derives from the Celtic 'spiced mead', and hydromel was a similar drink and, as its name implies, was made from honey and water.

When I visited Newlyn I found that the picturesque Meadery on the Coombe with the fairytale bridge across the stream was once a cinema and built 'Tudor' in the twenties. A fine restaurant sited there sells a wealth of mead in wine and liqueur varieties, appealingly put up in fancy glass bottles, decanters, barrels and jars. The sister meaderies, the Waterside and the Regent, Penzance, as well as the Trewellard, Pendeen (near St Just) follow suit. A fortress of a factory hidden behind the restaurant produces real mead made from wine and honey, but not the dry mead and not metheglin, the spiced kind. The demand is steady despite our changing taste from sweet to dry drinks. I wonder if those visitors buying fancy bottles for their friends realise how very good mead is to add to many dishes? The true honey flavour is one to be cherished today and used in preference to the ersatz essence that detracts from good food.

Mead Inspires Fruit

Most fruit dishes are enhanced by the addition of mead with the inevitable blob of Cornish cream on top, and/or dribbling of Cornish mead liqueur. And why not mead ice cream? Has any restaurant thought of making it?

Truly Cornish Cider?

A minor disappointment when I arrived in Cornwall was the lack of interest in cider or scrumpy (named from 'scrump', small apple). Questions at pubs and bottle stores elicited 'no call for it'. I also found difficulty in tracking down a truly Cornish cider made on local presses; so many — dry and sweet — seem to originate in Devon.

John's Cider Cup

Refreshing Summer Drink

When at last I tracked down a **truly** Cornish cider, made at Penryn by Mr John Watt and distributed throughout Britain as *Apple Blossom Scrumpy* by The Cornish Cider Co Ltd, I couldn't help enthusing about this delightfully fresh tasting drink (unfiltered and not carbonated). My reward was the following delicious cider cup recipe given me by the company's director.

2 litres *Apple Blossom Scrumpy*, 1 tablespoon brown sugar, 1 orange diced without any pith, ice cubes.

Cucumber slices may be added if liked but definitely nothing to overpower the flavour of the cider.

Cider, dry or sweet, as relevant, can replace wine in most recipes requiring wine or vinegar. I have enjoyed using it in many dishes, as will be noticed throughout this book. Yet here we fall so far short of our Breton cousins, who successfully developed their cider industry into a full variety of ciders, using their apple orchards to best advantage.

Cider Syllabub

In the old days bell ringers were reinforced with strong ale or cider to keep their 'feasten' bells going right merrily.

One old recipe for syllabub consisted of a pint of cider and a glass of brandy mixed with warm milk, which was poured from the spout of a large teapot held far above it. Naturally, the oldest of all syllabubs were milk milked directly from the cow into a basin of mead or metheglin — a frothy result without high pouring.

Cider Meat or Kiddley

This was made similarly to bread and milk, the cider replacing the milk. Honey was added and the 'cider mait' was eaten very hot. It was recommended to ease a cold.

Country Wine-Making

Home-made wines are an essential part of our cookery tradition and were created in various degrees of success and failure through hundreds of years from 'mother's knee' methods without the modern helps in the way of special yeast, fermentation lock or syphon tube. Nancy's sloe gin is an amusing example of dispensing with props — taking as she does, the gin bottle to the hedgerow! But because Boots have impressed me with their stacked shelves of reasonably priced equipment for home wine-making I am convinced that there must be an awful lot of people today, not labouring, but **enjoying** this hobby, using the fruits and vegetables from their gardens and the countryside.

The Cheapest Hobby?

And Most Rewarding

Apart from the complete beer and wine kits with all the basic needs for home brewing and fermentation a variety of yeasts is available, from the 'all-purpose' wine-making yeasts to specific types such as 'sherry' and 'champagne' — and the latter is useful for elderflowers, for example. Prices vary from the 18p packets sufficient for one fermentation of 5 litres — 30 litres (1—6 gallons) to those around 50p for 10 fermentations. The fermentaion locks are only about 30p and the syphon tube just a little over that. *Fining Gel* for clearing wine is also available for a few pence. As for the books on wine-making, Boots have a few but WH Smith and Sons have a wide range from 75p.

In Roseland, so many friends have given me their own recipes for home-made beers and wines that it almost breaks my heart not to find space for them in these pages. Nettle and ginger beers, dandelion, parsnip, carrot, rose petal, blackberry, turnip, cherry and those most popular of all, elderflower and elderberry wines, are still made; if not so frequently are the ciders and meads. Rose hip syrup, among the non-alcoholic health drinks, is important too and will certainly be included in a further book.

Ale and Beer

Daily drink of labourer and yeoman was a choice of cider or ale. With tea and coffee beyond the purse of most, one can understand the importance of ale for breakfast and supper, and children were brought up on it and their own 'small beer'. Despite the rude remarks about the Cornish beer of the past, Cecilia Fiennes commended our 'good bottled ale' when she visited the country in 1698.

What after all is good ale? A modern authority writes that the brewer should seek to achieve his own individual balance between malty sweetness and hoppy dryness and yeasty fruitfulness. The extent to which this balance is preserved in the pasteurised form depends on the care taken with that process. In the past hop gardens were leased out on the 'lives' system as were other orchards, and they were important to the life of the countryside. Today specialist breweries still make Cornish Ale and one (at Paradise Park, Hayle) even promotes sales by inviting the public to see the brewing process.

To Cook with Beer

Open 15 minutes before using to ensure it is not bubbly. Stale flat beer can be used. Beer is good for basting roasts, joints, poultry and chops, preferably dark beers for red meat and a pale lager for white meats. Fish can be poached or simmered in mild beer to which about a third as much vinegar has been added; with a bayleaf, juice and rind of a lemon the result is delicious. Gravies are enhanced in taste by using beer in proportion of 3—1 of other liquid.

Viticulture?

Perhaps my next book will enjoy publicising the rising growth of viticulture in the Duchy. One by one vineyards are being started with enthusiasm and faith in our climate.

Mahogony

Fisherman's Drink

This drink was a mixture of 1 part treacle and 2 parts gin, very well beaten together. Treacle was added to brandy and any liquor available, for similar strong drinks to revive or 'keep a man going in foul weather'.

Nancy's Sloe Gin

For a Good Year

Nancy's sloe gin is the best I have tasted but she points out 'I gave you a "good year" when plenty of sunshine caused the berries to be at their best and they were picked fully ripe and plump.'

She then demonstrated the result of a bad year with a 3-year-old bottle of a pallid brew, still drinkable however. She shortcuts the usual methods rather amusingly, using her basic recipe of ⅓ sloes, ⅓ sugar and ⅓ gin.

The empty former gin bottles (unwashed) are taken to the sloe hedges and the ripe sloes, with the bloom on them, are pulled from the stems sharply and dropped into the bottles, about one-third of each bottle. She says there is no need to prick the berries if you pick them off the stems exposing the natural opening at the end of each berry. When home she funnels over the berries one-third sugar and shakes the bottle until sugar is dissolved, and a good colour. Then she tops up each bottle with gin to within 2″ of the top of the neck of each bottle. They are then corked and left to ferment naturally. The bottles are shaken at intervals. (An old custom practised by man and wife at the fireside of an evening was to roll the bottles between them with their feet!) The wine is better if kept for a year or more but, if needed, say, for Christmas, it may be drunk before. To serve, strain into a decanter and allow to settle.

Hedgerow Fruits and Herbs

Those interested in this fascinating subject will find all the answers in Richard Mabey's *Food for Free* (Fontana/Collins 1975). The author gives the description and recipes for an amazing number of edible plants to be culled from fields and hedgerows. A smaller book *Free for All* by Ceres (Thorson's) is also of value.

HERBS AND PICKLES

But a Few Words

Old cook books include herbs as a vital ingredient in many recipes, even as a substitution for meat. The kiddleywink broth is an example. Vegetables cooked in the stockpot with scraps of meat and herbs were an essential part of our folk cooking. Perhaps that is why some people object to the quick 'crisp' cooking of vegetables offered in the best restaurants. 'They only half cook their veges' is a common complaint of oldsters today.

Spinach was important with sorrel, to which were added, as available, parsley, beet leaves, mustard and cress, lettuce, borage, chives, garlic and onion. After blanching and draining they were chopped up finely, seasoned and spread into a buttered dish. A batter was placed over and the pudding put into a moderate oven until the top was baked.

Today the greenstuffs mentioned, together with the tops and left-over outer leaves of other vegetables are quickly translated by means of a small liquidiser into soups and sauces.

The art of cooking with herbs is learned by judgement and experimentation. A dish is spoiled by strong herbs overpowering the flavours of others. Sweet herbs, so often mentioned in old recipes, consist of a few sprigs of parsley, one of lemon thyme and one bay leaf. Or alternatively, 2 sprigs of parsley, one of sweet marjoram, one of winter savoury and one of lemon thyme. If tied securely with a long thread they can easily be removed at the end of cooking and before the soup or gravy is thickened.

Caper Sauces

Instead of the traditional rich caper sauces made with butter or cream the capers may be added to a white sauce in which a tablespoon of butter or cream has been stirred. The capers or 'mock' capers should be added to the sauce with a little wine vinegar. If the caper sauce is to be served with fish a little anchovy paste may be added too. Instead of capers tiny pieces of gherkin and even parsley (after boiling) were used.

To Dry Summer Herbs

Gather the herbs on a dry day, just before they begin to flower. Cut off any roots, cleanse thoroughly, spread them out on a tray to dry in a warm place, and fairly quickly. The sun is best but they may be dried in a moderate oven taking care they do not burn.

Fresh herbs, growing on the kitchen window ledge, always at hand, are a boon for the discriminating cook. Dried herbs simply cannot compete in flavour.

Fresh Herb Vinegars

No Need to Buy

Wine vinegar is excellent for the creation of flavoured vinegars. Use small screw-top bottles for a family, or for two, those small empty glass jars with secure lids used for dried herbs. Place a fresh piece of any herb inside, fill up with vinegar, secure the lid and leave to use as needed for salad dressings, sauces, soups and stuffings. Sorrel, fennel, thyme, chervil, marjoram and cut garlic cloves (the latter peeled) impart their own distinctive fragrance to the liquid; for this reason it is best not to mix the herbs in the various bottles. You can create any alliance with the flavoured vinegars themselves. Keep jars in fridge.

Pickled Fruits

Nobody thought of buying pickles in Granny's day. They were so easily made, as they are now. Make pickle from any fruit abundantly in season and have pickles the year round, providing acceptable gifts, too, for your friends. The basic pickling liquid is:

> 1 tablespoon good curry powder, 2 teaspoons turmeric, a few cloves, 1 red pepper (chopped), salt, pepper and a teaspoon of sugar boiled with 1½ bottles dark wine vinegar.

Lay fruit on a sugared board then combine with the hot spiced vinegar in sterilised jars. A chilli or two or bay leaf may be added, or slices of onion, as taste dictates. Using this basic recipe go on experimenting until you make fruit pickle to your liking, sweet or sour as required.

Pickle any fruits. Select fruits that are dry, fresh and not over ripe. The following are excellent pickled. Pears: peel, core and quarter. Peaches: skin and halve. Apricots: leave whole unless large. Plums: leave whole or halve and stone. Crab apples: do not peel or core. But if ordinary sharp apples are used peel, core and cut into thick slices.

Mock Capers

From Nasturtium Pods

Imitation capers can be made from nasturtium seeds. Leave fairly young green seeds in salt and water for an hour. Strain. Bring a fresh lot of salt and water to the boil and cook seeds in it for 2 minutes. Place in jar, cover with spiced vinegar, seal and store in a cool place. Some old recipes included peppercorns, horse-radish or cloves and leaves of tarragon — which actually added up to a sort of pickle.

What is MSG?

For those readers unacquainted with monosodium glutamate used as an ingredient in some recipes: MSG is of cereal origin with a slightly mushroom flavour that has been used in Japan and China for centuries to enhance the flavour of savoury foods. Today it will be found under various brand names or combined with food flavourings on supermarket 'spice' shelves. It is sprinkled like salt over fish, meat and vegetable dishes — but not egg dishes or fruits. Arguments that arise from time to time about the misuse of MSG do not appear to influence professional chefs who use it traditionally, with discretion, in **small** quantities. As scientists have pointed out MSG is a natural substance allied to an acid found in the human body and is not an artificial product — such as are the cyclamates.

If MSG is not available at your supermarket it may be purchased from some delicatessen stores. Use it from a salt dispenser as required in cooking, but **not** on the table for use as salt.

Allspice and Mixed Spice

Some old recipes confuse allspice with mixed spice. Allspice is, of course, pimento and in no way connected with mixed spice.

THE COOKERY REVOLUTION

Air . . . But Not All Hot Air

Soul food, referred to in an earlier book, is but one of the more mundane happenings of today. More important is the revolution started by some chefs in France in about 1974 led by Michel Guérard. This daring artist of *La Grande Cuisine Francaise* maintains one should be able to eat well without getting fat. Guérard calls the new cookery movement of his *la cuisine minceur*, after *mince*, meaning slim. His finesse in producing fine dishes with far less calories than their names suggest attracted discriminating people to his modest *Pot au Feu* in Asnieres, an industrial suburb of Paris. At time of writing he owns several catering establishments and many chefs throughout the world are following his methods under the label *nouvelle cuisine*.

Pure Air

What exactly is this sweet smell of success? As one writer put it 'pure air'. Let's explain. One of his most successful ingredients is air rhythmically whipped into soups, sauces and vegetables; they are beaten into a light foam without the addition of butter and cream. Veal, marinated and basted with orange and lemon juice, is cooked with tarragon sauce. Sea fish is cooked with seaweed. He has discovered new tastes such as spinach combined with a purée of pears instead of cream. He uses yoghurt instead of butter and cream in many recipes. One recipe of his reminds me of my endeavours to cook without fats and water. For example, he says he had always made his *saumon a l'oseille* (salmon with sorrel) with butter. He experimented and today he cooks the salmon in an iron pan: 'the fish is just as pink and the taste truer', he says, translated from the French. It is this true taste of food I have tried to give you in my planned recipes. And of course among my household pets is that important iron pan: those old-time virtues valued yet again: it diffuses the heat evenly, doesn't buckle and will not burn. If you treat it nicely and clean with salt and paper it need never rust. An alternative to the iron pans is our own Cornish crock and other earthenware utensils.

Another Revolution

It is recorded how when Cromwell had sacked a village in Britain the surviving inhabitants were left with nothing, not even one iron pot in which to do their cooking. Then someone found a soldier's helmet and this was handed round from house to house as a stewing pot for the whole village.

What does the future hold for us? Whatever befalls fortunately we will know how to cook superbly at little cost . . . in an iron pot — or a Cornish crock.

MEASURE FOR MEASURE

Both Imperial and Metric measures are given in these pages. They are not equivalents and therefore not interchangeable. Avoid mixing Imperial and Metric measures in the same recipe.

As mentioned at the beginning of this book, not being a standard instructional cook book, cups and spoons, without the Metric equivalent are given as originally printed in this anthology of recipes old and new.

While Metric excludes spoons, for easier reading we have given them in preference to ml but refer to the table below. The cup mentioned in the older home recipes usually referred to breakfast cup size (about 200 ml), while a teacup is about 160 ml. You will find three breakfast cups (not mugs) will fill your pint milk bottle which is marked 568 ml. The standard cup measure used in our modern recipes is equivalent to 250 ml or 300 ml (½ pint). The alternative 300 ml has been used because it is nearer to the Metric contents of the milk bottle — which is actually a valuable measure for liquids in your kitchen.

Cups

1 cup	250 ml OR	300 ml (½ pint)
2 cups	500 ml OR	600 ml (1 pint)
3 cups	750 ml OR	900 ml (1½ pints)
4 cups	1000 ml OR	1200 ml (1 litre)

Teaspoons

¼ teaspoon	1.0 ml
½ teaspoon	2.5 ml
1 teaspoon	5.0 ml
1 dessertspoon	10.0 ml
2 teaspoons	10.0 ml
1 tablespoon	15.0 ml
2 tablespoons	30.0 ml

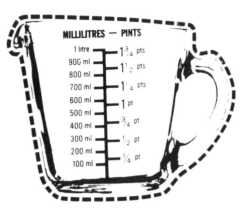

MILLILITRES — PINTS

1 litre	1¾ pts
900 ml	1½ pts
800 ml	
700 ml	1¼ pts
600 ml	1 pt
500 ml	
400 ml	¾ pt
300 ml	½ pt
200 ml	
100 ml	¼ pt

TO TEST OVEN TEMPERATURES

Granny's Way

Failing a thermometer, you can test heat by placing a piece of white paper in the oven. A very hot oven will turn the paper golden brown in 1 minute (230°C; 450°F or Gas 8). A hot oven will turn the paper golden brown in 3 minutes (200°C; 400°F or Gas 6). A moderate oven will turn paper golden brown in 5 minutes (180°C—190°C; 350°F—375°F or Gas 4—5). A slow oven will turn paper golden brown in 7 minutes (100°C—150°C; 200°F—300°F or Gas ½—2).

Acknowledgements

With a limited time at my disposal I have milked many people's cows (killing off a few sacred ones, I fear) to produce what I hope is some good butter, or better still, genuine Cornish cream. The expression about milking cows is yet another adapted from AK Hamilton Jenkin's *Cornish Homes and Customs*, published in 1933 by JM Dent and Sons Ltd, with later publishing rights acquired by David and Charles. This and two other books, namely Nora Chadwick's *Early Brittany* (University of Wales Press 1969) and that oft-quoted *Cornish Recipes, Ancient and Modern*, compiled by Edith Martin (AW Jordon, Printer, Truro) in 1929 and issued by the Cornwall Federation of Women's Institutes, have been perhaps the most helpful of the many books I have read concerning our Cornish past.

My thanks are due particularly to the British Museum; Professor Charles Thomas, Institute of Cornish Studies, University of Exeter; Mr HL Douch, Curator of Cornwall County Museum, Truro; Mr FGR Thorn, Curator of Bude Museum; Mrs MA Evans, for the Curator, Mr LM Pole, Saffron Walden Museum; Mr G Clotworthy, Information Officer, National Trust, Lanhydrock; Mr Laurence O'Toole and Miss KN Bowring, among other authors credited in these pages.

For some of my basic knowledge of cooking and the testing of recipes, as always, I am indebted to my friend Mrs Lesley Faull (*Commandeur Associé de la Commanderie des Cordons Bleus de France*; *Chevalier de la Confrérie des Chevaliers du Tastevin*). The late Mr André L Simon, CBE, MM, was the first patron when she opened her school, Silwood Kitchen, at Cape Town in 1966.

Business firms who have helped me with information are: Shell UK Ltd; Mr Ian Greet, Falmouth Fish Selling Co Ltd; Mr Nick Howell, Newlyn; C Shippam Ltd; Mr ST Leiworthy, Cornish Mead Co Ltd; Mr John Watt, The Cornish Cider Co; The Manager,

Liptons, Truro; Mr Richard Harris, Fowey's Sea Products; Mr DEG Hills, Truro Pottery and Old Kiln Museum; Mr Michael Green, The Real Ale and Cheese Shop, Truro; Mr Martyn Melhuish, SW correspondent for *Fishing News*.

My Roseland 'cookery friends', mentioned by Christian name only in these pages, include Mrs Shirley Green (who also helped me with typing), Mrs Mavis Wilson, Mrs Joan Tomlinson, Mrs Marion Badcock, Mrs Doreen Stein (for advice and transport), my cousin Miss Nancy Hearle whose parents farmed at Tregassick and Mr DL Clark, for one item from his fund of old stories.

I am indebted also to the Comtesse du Merle and Miss Zorig Andcott for information on Brittany today, and Mr and Mrs GG Berry for books.

Other sources of information are mentioned with the relevant text.

Index

Lamb, 55
Lamb's Tongue (with Almond Sauce), 69
Lamprey, 34
Lard, 50
Leeky Pasties, 76
Likky Pie, 81
Limpets, 37
Little Liver Cakes, 69
Liver (Poor Man's Goose), 68
Lobster, 42
Lobster (or Crab) Thermidor, 44
Looe, 27

Mackerel, 23, 24 Pâté, 24 Smoked, 24 Marinated (Soused), 23
Margarine, 90
Mahogany, 8, 125
Marinade for Pilchards, 22 Venison, 63 Sweetbreads, 67
Marika Hanbury Tenison, 99
Martin (Edith), 134
Mavis' Saffron Cake, 102
Mead, 122
Meaty Fuggan, 72
Metheglin, 122
Metric and Imperial Measures, 11, 132
Mevagissey Ducks, 21
Michel Guérard, 130
Milk Puddings, 92
Millers (of Corn), 111
Minced Meat (Basic Mix), 59
Mock Capers, 129
Mock Crab Cocktail, 31
Monkfish, 31
Morgay Soup, 14
Mousehole, 21
Muggety Pie, 77
Mullet, 26
Mussels, 37
Mussels à la Mariniere, 38
Mussel and Spinach Sandwich, 38
Mutton, 55
MSG (Monosodium Glutamate), 129

Nancy's (Home), 103 Scallops, 40 Sloe Gin, 126
Nasturtium Seeds (Substitute for Capers), 129
Nuns Excommunicated, 43

Octopus, 47
Offal, 66
Ogee, 71

NOTES

NOTES